Canada's Lan

Grades 1-3

Written by Ruth Solski
Illustrated by S&S Learning Materials

ISBN 1-55035-738-7
Canada's Landmarks, SSJ1-51
Copyright 2003 S&S Learning Materials
15 Dairy Avenue
Napanee, Ontario
K7R 1M4
All Rights Reserved * Printed in Canada
A Division of the Solski Group

Permission to Reproduce
Permission is granted to the individual teacher who purchases one copy of this book to reproduce the student activity material for use in his/her classroom only. Reproduction of these materials for an entire school or for a school system, or for other colleagues or for commercial sale is **strictly prohibited**. No part of this publication may be transmitted in any form or by any means, electronic, mechanical, recording or otherwise without the prior written permission of the publisher. "We acknowledge the financial support of the Government of Canada through the Book Publishing Industry Development program for our publishing activities."

Published in Canada by:
S&S Learning Materials
15 Dairy Avenue
Napanee, Ontario
K7R 1M4
www.sslearning.com

Look For OTHER CANADIAN UNITS

Item #	Title	Gr.
SSJ1-01	Canada	Gr. 1
J1-02	All About Canada	2
J1-03	Let's Visit Canada	3
J1-04	Canadian Provinces	3-6
J1-11	Wild Animals of Canada	2-3
J1-12	Famous Canadians	4-8
J1-13	Let's Look at Canada	4-6
J1-23	Ottawa	7-9
J1-32	What is Canada?	P-K
J1-33	Canadian Capital Cities	4-6
J1-35	Toronto	4-8
J1-37	Canadian Arctic Inuit	2-3
J1-38	Canadian Provinces and Territories	4-6
J1-39	Canadian Government	5-8
J1-40	Development of Western Canada	7-8
J1-41	Canada and It's Trading Partners	6-8
J1-42	Canada's Traditions and Celebrations	1-3
J1-45	Fathers of Confederation	4-8
J1-46	Canadian Industries	4-6
J1-47	Prime Ministers of Canada	4-8
J1-48	Canada's Landmarks	4-6
J1-49	Elections in Canada	4-8
J1-50	Amazing Facts in Canadian History	4-6
J1-51	Canada's Landmarks	1-3

Let's Visit...

J1-14	Let's Visit Saskatchewan	2-4
J1-15	Let's Visit British Columbia	2-4
J1-16	Let's Visit Alberta	2-4
J1-17	Let's Visit Ontario	2-4
J1-18	Let's Visit Manitoba	2-4
J1-19	Let's Visit Prince Edward Island	2-4
J1-20	Let's Visit Nova Scotia	2-4
J1-21	Let's Visit New Brunswick	2-4
J1-27	Let's Visit Newfoundland and Labrador	2-4
J1-28	Let's Visit Yukon Territory	2-4
J1-30	Let's Visit Northwest Territory	2-4
J1-31	Let's Visit Québec	2-4
J1-34	Let's Visit Nunavut	2-4

Discover Canada

J1-22	Discover Québec	5-7
J1-24	Discover Prince Edward Island	5-7
J1-25	Discover Ontario	5-7
J1-26	Discover Nova Scotia	5-7
J1-36	Discover Nunavut Territory	5-7

Canadian Communities

J1-05	Farming Community	3-4
J1-06	Fishing Community	3-4
J1-07	Mining Community	3-4
J1-08	Lumbering Community	3-4
J1-09	Ranching Community	3-4
J1-10	Inuit Community	3-4

Published by:
S&S Learning Materials
15 Dairy Avenue
Napanee, Ontario
K7R 1M4

All rights reserved.
Printed in Canada.

Canada's Landmarks

Table of Contents

Introduction to Teachers	4
Reproducible Booklet Cover	5
Cape Spear Lighthouse	6
L'Anse aux Meadows	8
Gros Morne National Park	10
Green Gables	12
Province House	14
Acadian Historical Village	16
Kings Landing Historical Settlement	18
The Hartland Covered Bridge	20
Fundy Bay and the Hopewell Rocks	22
Alexander Graham Bell National Historic Park	24
Halifax Citadel National Historic Site	26
Peggy's Cove	28
Montmorency Falls Park	33
Quebec City	32
Percé Rock	34
Niagara Falls	36
Ste. Marie Among the Hurons	40
The CN Tower	42
Mennonite Heritage Village	44
York Factory National Historic Site	46
The Big Muddy Badlands	48
World's Largest Tomahawk	50
Giant Easter Egg	52
Badlands and Bones	54
Head-Smashed-In Buffalo Jump	56
Barkerville Historic Town	58
Queen Charlotte Islands	60
Vancouver's Bridges	62
Stern-wheelers of the Far North	64
Nahanni National Park	66
Yellowknife	68
Iqaluit: Capital of Nunavut	70
Auyuittuq National Park	72
Famous Cabins of the North	74
Answer Key	77

© S&S Learning Materials

Canada's Landmarks

Introduction to Teachers

Canada's Landmarks provides information and follow-up activities on various landmarks located in Canada. The main objective of the material in this book is to familiarize and to broaden students' knowledge with the location and historical aspects of heritage sites and tourist attractions found throughout their country. With this knowledge, deeper feelings of pride and patriotism will be fostered.

The information provided is for the teacher so that he/she may become better acquainted with each landmark. The landmark could then be discussed and located with the students. The activity provided for each landmark may be used as a listening and reading follow-up, and may have to be teacher-directed depending on the students' abilities.

The various reading and listening skills such as noting and recalling details, recalling events and information, sequencing, context clues, vocabulary development, and comprehending oral information have been implemented. Research skills may be developed through the use of the open-ended reproducible activity page. The various activities completed may be compiled in a booklet using the reproducible cover page entitled "Canada's Landmarks". The information and activities may be worked on in any order and may be used by the teacher in the format that best suits the needs of the students.

A mapping centre could be established on a table in the classroom. On the table, place a portable bulletin board. Tack a large map of Canada to the bulletin board. As each landmark is discussed, mark its location with a labelled flag attached to a straight pin.

Example:

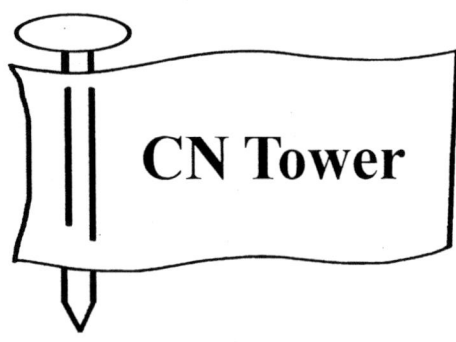

Place brochures and pamphlets pertaining to various canadian landmarks at the mapping centre for student viewing.

Have fun making a trip across our beautiful land with your students!

Canada's Landmarks

Name: _____

Information

Cape Spear Lighthouse

A Newfoundland and Labrador Landmark

Cape Spear Lighthouse

The first lighthouses were burning bonfires located on the ends of points of land at harbour entrances. Later, these lights were replaced by towers with fire beacons on the top. Candles, oil lamps, and eventually kerosene lamps were used as beacons in the early 1800s.

In 1835, a lighthouse was built on the most easterly point of land in North America. It stood on **Cape Spear** in Newfoundland and its light directed ships into St. John's Harbour. Cape Spear is closer to Warsaw, Poland, than it is to Vancouver, British Columbia. The Cape Spear Lighthouse stands 75 metres tall and is Newfoundland's oldest surviving lighthouse.

The **Cape Spear Lighthouse** has flashed its message to ships and mariners since the mid 1800s. The original building was a square, two-storey structure with the light tower itself in the middle of it. In September 1836, its light was in operation. In 1878, a fog horn was installed to guide ships into St. John's Harbour.

The first light came from another lighthouse in Scotland. The light rays came from seven burners and were intensified by curved reflectors. The lamps and reflectors were held on a metal frame which rotated slowly to produce a seventeen-second flash of light, followed by 43 seconds of darkness. The movement of the light was controlled by a clock-like mechanism. The Cape Spear light underwent many changes down through the years and in 1930, it was operated by electricity.

During the Second World War, Cape Spear became a coastal defence battery, equipped with two fifteen centimetre guns to be used to protect the entrance to St. John's Harbour from German submarines and raiders off the coast of the island. The guns were built at the tip of Cape Spear and were connected by underground passageways to the magazine (storage for ammunition) and equipment rooms. Troops were stationed here from 1941-1945 and barracks, mess halls, and canteens were built. At the end of the war, most of the buildings were demolished except for the gun emplacements which remind us of a sombre period in our military history.

Today, Cape Spear Lighthouse has been restored to its original appearance and refurnished as a lightkeeper's residence to the period of 1839. The bunkers and the gun emplacements provide an excellent view of the ocean where visitors search the horizon for whales, icebergs, seabirds, and ships heading in and out of the St. John's Harbour.

Activity   Name: _____

Cape Spear

A Newfoundland and Labrador Landmark

Use the words in the box to complete the story about Cape Spear.

Print the words on the lines provided.

Cape Spear Lighthouse

Early lighthouses were large _____ built at the openings to large _____ They were built to _____ ships _____ and to _____ them of _____ in the water.

Next, men built _____ with fire _____ on the top. _____, _____, and _____ were used as beacons in early lighthouses.

A _____ was built on _____ in Newfoundland in 1835. It was built to guide ships and seamen into _____ Harbour. The Cape Spear Lighthouse stands _____ metres tall and is a _____ two-storey building with the light _____ in the middle of it. At first, its light was lit by kerosene and then _____. Its light _____ on for seventeen seconds and off for 43 seconds.

During World War Two, Canadian _____ were stationed at Cape Spear in an underground _____ for four years. Two large _____ were built at the _____ of Cape Spear to _____ St. John's Harbour from _____ submarines.

Today, tourists visit the lighthouse and the underground bunkers and search the ocean for _____, _____, _____, and _____.

bonfires	guide	safely	dangers	openings
warn	Candles	beacons	towers	oil lamps
harbours	kerosene	square	lighthouse	Cape Spear
75	St. John's	electricity	tower	flashed
soldiers	bunker	protect	tip	whales
German	seabirds	ships	guns	icebergs

Information

L'Anse aux Meadows
A Newfoundland and Labrador Landmark

Nearly 1 000 years ago **Leif Eiriksson**, a Viking explorer, and a crew of 30 men anchored in an inviting bay somewhere along the coast of North America 300 years before Christopher Columbus discovered America. When the men stepped ashore, they discovered a low and rolling landscape covered with lush meadows and thick forests. A small stream flowed from a nearby lake. Spectacular tides amazed them and when the tide went out, the entire bay became dry land.

The Viking explorers were delighted with what they saw. They decided to set up camp on the shore. Short trips into the country made them realize how rich this country was. An abundance of salmon lived in the many streams. There was plenty of timber located in the thick forests and the climate was so mild the grass stayed green all year. One day, a crew member wandered from the settlement and discovered grapes growing wild in the forest. After this exciting discovery, Leif Eiriksson called the new land "Vinland", Land of Wine.

Eiriksson and his men returned to Greenland the next summer. Their ship was heavily loaded with a cargo of timber and grapes in the form of wine or raisins. The people in Greenland were happy to see the timber since they had no timber suitable for building.

The news of Eiriksson's successful trip aroused the interest of other Greenlanders. **Thorfinn Karlsefni**, an Icelandic trader decided to make an expedition to Vinland. His expedition may have had 135 men, and fifteen women, livestock, and three or more ships. The same camp established by Eiriksson was used and the Vikings spent several summers exploring the land and collecting lumber, pelts and other things that could be sold in Greenland or Europe.

Eventually the Vikings met the Native people who lived on the land. They were called "Skraelings" by the Vikings. In time, the Skraelings and the Vikings clashed. The Vikings returned to Greenland as they were greatly outnumbered by the natives and feared for their lives.

On one of the voyages by either Leif Eiriksson or Thorfinn Karlsefni, the explorers settled for a time at the head of Newfoundland's Great Northern Peninsula at a place called **L'Anse aux Meadows.**

In this area, they built a small community on a narrow gravel terrace close to a water-logged peat bog and a small stream. No one knows how long they stayed but they lived there long enough to build houses, workshops and a small forge. At this forge, iron was smelted for the first time in the New World. The buildings decayed and nature reclaimed the land after they left.

In 1960, a Norwegian explorer and writer **Helge Ingstad**, came upon the site at L'Anse aux Meadows. It took Helge and his wife, archaeologist Anne Stine Ingstad, and an international team of archaeologists from Norway, Iceland, Sweden and the United States eight years to excavate the site. They found the lower parts of the walls of eight Viking buildings from the 11th century. The walls and roof had been made of sod laid over a framework of wood. These buildings were the same as the ones used in Iceland and Greenland just before and after the year 1000. In the middle of the floor of each building was a long, narrow fireplace used for heating, lighting and cooking.

Near the site today, sod houses have been recreated and the artifacts discovered are on display. In 1977, L'Anse aux Meadows was decleared a National Historic Site and is cared for by Parks Canada. In 1978, the site was declared a United Nations World Heritage Site.

Activity

Name: _____

L'Anse aux Meadows

A Newfoundland and Labrador Landmark

L'Anse aux Meadows

L'Anse aux Meadows is a favourite tourist attraction in Newfoundland and Labrador.

Use the words in the box to complete the story about L'Anse aux Meadows.

Print the words on the lines provided.

Many years ago, Leif Eiriksson, a _____, and his men _____ and _____ in parts of North America. They camped somewhere along the _____ of North America 300 years before Christopher _____ discovered America. Eiriksson and his men found this new land to be rich in _____, _____ and wild _____.

Other Vikings heard of Eiriksson's successful _____ and _____ to this new land. Some Vikings built a _____ on Newfoundland's Great Northern peninsula at a place called L'Anse aux _____. Here they built houses and workshops from wood and _____. A _____ was built to smelt _____ for the first time in North America. In time, the Vikings returned to _____ and the buildings _____ and the place became _____ with plants.

Helge Ingstad, his wife and a group of archaeologists excavated the _____ at L'Anse aux Meadows for _____ years. They discovered the _____ parts of the _____ of eight buildings and other artifacts at the site.

Near the site today stands a _____ Viking Community. There are sod and timber _____ and artifacts on display. In 1977, L'Anse aux Meadows was declared a National _____ Site. In 1978, it became a United Nations _____ Site.

Viking	Columbus	salmon	Meadows	Heritage	lived	coast
re-created	timber	community	houses	trip	lower	Historic
grapes	travelled	explored	walls	rotted	Greenland	
forge	overgrown	eight	sod	iron	site	

© S&S Learning Materials

9

SSJ1-51

Information

Gros Morne National Park

A Newfoundland and Labrador Landmark

Gros Morne National Park

Gros Morne National Park is located on the western shore of the Great Northern Peninsula of Newfoundland. The park is 1 805 sq kilometres in size, the largest national park in Atlantic Canada, and contains the most spectacular scenery in Canada's national park system.

The Long Range Mountains rise abruptly from the narrow coastal plain and dominate the park's landscape. At the top of these mountains is a vast alpine plateau of tundra, bogs and "tuckamoor" (tangled, twisted thickets of stunted spruce and fir trees). Gros Morne is one of the few places in the world where rocks from the earth's mantle and oceanic crust are exposed, providing an outstanding example of major stages in the earth's evolutionary history. This orange-brown rock is 500 million years old and is a huge slab of oceanic crust and underlying mantle rock that was forced to the surface when the continents of Africa and North America collided.

The coastal lowlands have large, raised bogs dotted with pitcher plants. The Gulf of St. Lawrence shoreline is very picturesque with rocky capes and peninsulas jutting into the ocean and broad, sandy beaches. The towering cliffs of freshwater fiords carved by glaciers are spectacular land forms. Other important water bodies in the park are Western Brook Pond, Trout River Pond, Ten Mile Pond, Bonne Bay, St. Paul's Inlet, Lomond River and Bakers Brook Falls.

There are over 40 sites rich in ancient fossils such as trilobites and exposed rock strata in Gros Morne National Park. Two distinct ecoregions are found in the park. They are the coastal lowlands along the Gulf of St. Lawrence and the alpine plateau of the Long Range Mountains. These areas are home to moose, red foxes, black bears, snowshoe hares, herds of woodland caribou, ptarmigans, bald eagles and ospreys. Harbour seals breed on small islands off the coast and whales can be seen migrating.

Tourists from all over the world come to the Gros Morne National Park to hike the various trails, view the beautiful scenery, observe the wildlife, look at some of the oldest rock found in the world or to hunt for fossils and watch the 10 000 year old icebergs floating in the ocean.

Activity Name: _____

Gros Morne National Park

A Newfoundland and Labrador Landmark

Gros Morne National Park

Gros Morne National Park is a popular park visited by tourists from all over the world.

Choose words from the box that will complete the story about Gros Morne National Park.

Print the words on the lines provided.

    Gros Morne National Park is the _____ one in Atlantic Canada. It is found on the _____ shore of the Great Northern Peninsula in _____. Mountains, _____, capes, _____ and freshwater _____ are land forms found in the park.

    Some of the _____ rock in the world can be seen in Gros Morne. This orange-brown rock is 500 _____ years old. It was made when the oceanic crust and underlying mantle rock was _____ to the surface when the _____ of Africa and North America _____. Fossils such as _____ are found in many places.

    Wildlife such as _____, red _____, black _____, snowshoe _____, herds of woodland _____, ptarmigan, bald _____ and _____ make their homes in the park. Harbour _____ and migrating _____ can be seen in the ocean.

    _____ travel to Gros Morne National Park to _____ the many trails, to _____ the beautiful scenery, to _____ the wildlife, to _____ at some of the oldest rock, to _____ for fossils or to _____ 10 000 year old _____ floating in the ocean.

icebergs	hunt	photograph	whales	watch	look
Tourists	osprey	trilobites	observe	bears	hike
collided	seals	squeezed	moose	hares	foxes
fiords	million	continents	oldest	valleys	largest
western	peninsulas	Newfoundland	caribou	eagles	

© S&S Learning Materials

Information

Green Gables

A Prince Edward Island Landmark

Green Gables

Green Gables is the home that Lucy Maud Montgomery used as the setting for her well known novel - "Anne of Green Gables". The house and farm is located in Prince Edward Island National Park close to the town of Cavendish. It was built in the mid-1800's and was owned by David and Margaret MacNeill, who were cousins of Lucy Maud Montgomery's grandfather.

Green Gables is the home in which the characters Marilla and Mathew Cuthbert and Anne Shirley lived. In 1937, the farmland was preserved by the Federal Government within Prince Edward Island National Park. The famous green and white victorian house has been restored and furnished the way it would have been in Anne's day. In Anne's room, there are artifacts from the story, including a slate like the one Anne used to crack over Gilbert Blyth's head. This house is a living monument to the Anne of Green Gables book.

At the Green Gables site, period farm outbuildings have been restored such as a barn, granary, and woodshed. The famous trails are well signed and those who walk them will surely hear echoes of Anne Shirley's voice.

Although Lucy Maud Montgomery never lived at Green Gables, she lived nearby with her grandparents. She explored the farm and surrounding woodlands and knew them well. She discovered places and gave them names such as "Lover's Lane", "Haunted Woods", and "Balsam Hollow".

Every summer, thousands of tourists from all over the world stroll through the humble green and white frame house and follow the trails through the shady forest while listening to the babbling brook of Lucy Maud Montgomery's childhood.

Activity   Name: _____

Green Gables

A Prince Edward Island Landmark

Anne of Green Gables

Green Gables is a house that is well known by children all over the world. It has become famous because of a book called "Anne of Green Gables".

Read the story about Green Gables and complete the sentences with the missing words.

Print the words on the lines provided.

In Prince Edward Island National Park is a famous house called _____ Gables. This is the house that Lucy Maud Montgomery used as the _____ for her book called _____ of Green _____. The green and _____ frame _____ has been _____ and _____ the way it would have looked when Anne lived in it.

A _____, granary, and _____ have been restored as well. All of the famous places talked about in the book are well marked. They are the _____ Woods, Lover's _____ and Balsam _____.

Although Lucy Maud Montgomery _____ lived at Green Gables, she _____ up nearby and had _____ the farm and surrounding woods and knew them well.

Today, _____ come from all over the world to _____ Green Gables and to _____ the _____ found in the haunted woods.

trails	furnished	house	setting	Anne	woodshed
Green	Haunted	white	explored	grew	never
walk	restored	Lane	tourists	Gables	Hollow
visit	barn				

© S&S Learning Materials   13   SSJ1-51

Information

Province House

A Prince Edward Island Landmark

Province House

The most impressive building on Prince Edward Island is **Province House** in Charlottetown. It was completed in 1847. A local architect, by the name of Isaac Smith, designed and built the building. Province House was built to accomodate the Provincial Legislature and administrative offices. It still plays an important role in the Island's public life with the assembly still holding sessions here.

Province House is a neo-classical three-storey building made with Wallace stone from Nova Scotia. It is now a National Historical Site. Many tourists stop here to visit the restored and refurnished legislative council chamber, library and other offices. Tour guides share many stories and facts with the people that visit.

In September 1864, Province House was the scene of the first conference on colonial union. Delegates from the colonies of Prince Edward Island, New Brunswick, Nova Scotia, and Canada met in the legislative chamber now called the Confederation Chamber to begin discussions which led to Confederation in 1867. Prince Edward Island has the historic importance as the "cradle of Confederation" and Charlottetown is known as the "birthplace of Canada".

Fathers of Confederation

Activity Name: _____

Province House

A Prince Edward Island Landmark

Province House

Canada's story as a country began in a tall, stone building called **Province House** in Prince Edward Island.

Read the story about Province House and complete the sentences with the missing words found in the flag.

Print the words on the line provided.

_____ is a very important building in the city of _____ on Prince Edward _____. It was _____ to provide a place where the province's _____ could meet.

   Province House is a _____ building made with a special _____ from Nova Scotia. Many years ago, it was used to hold the first _____ about _____ all the _____ to make one big _____. This is called _____. Charlottetown is often referred to as "the _____ of Canada".

_____ visit Province House to _____ the council chambers, the library and other offices.

Province House	built	stone
Charlottetown	government	conference
Island	three-storey	joining
confederation	birthplace	Tourists
view	provinces	country

© S&S Learning Materials   15   SSJ1-51

Information

Acadian Historical Village
(Village Historique Acadien)
A New Brunswick Landmark

An Acadian Historical Village

In New Brunswick, on the banks of the Rivière du Nord, near the town of Caraquet lies an **Acadian Historical Village**. The Acadians were the early French settlers who came with Champlain and called the land they worked "Acadie". The village reflects the Acadian way of life experienced during 1770-1890. There are 50 buildings in the Village that are original and made from roughly hewn timbers. The homes are usually one large room with an attic or loft used for storage. The large room was used by the entire family for working, eating and sleeping. The homes are furnished with only the necessities and display the poverty and hardships endured by the very early French settlers.

The Acadian Historical Village is staffed with bilingual interpreters, dressed in period costumes, who bring customs and traditional trades back to life in original buildings. The Village has a copper's shop, a lobster hatchery, a tinsmith shop, a covered bridge, and the Château Albert, which is a hotel where tourists can spend the night. The interpreters spin, weave, hammer hot metals on a forge, and set type for a newspaper. Grain is grown on low land reclaimed from the sea by a dyking system developed by early French settlers.

Horse-drawn carts take tourists past many sights displaying the Acadians' tale of their struggle to survive after their expulsion by the British.

An Acadian Woman

Activity Name: _____

Acadian Historical Village
A New Brunswick Landmark

The **Acadian Historic Village** near Caraquet, New Brunswick shows people how early French settlers lived many years ago.

Read the story about the Acadian Historic Village and complete the sentences with the missing words in the box.

Print the words on the lines provided.

Acadians were early _____ settlers who came to the new _____ with Samuel de Champlain. They called this new land _____.

In _____, on the banks of the Rivière du Nord, near the town of _____, is an Acadian Historical Village. The _____ and the _____ show how early settlers lived and the hardships they suffered.

There are _____ buildings in the Village. They are made from roughly cut _____. An Acadian home was _____ large room with a _____ used to store things. The large room was used for _____, _____, and _____. The Acadians were _____ and had little _____. Women wearing Acadian costumes _____, _____ and _____ Acadian food for the other workers in the Village. They also _____ tourists and _____ their questions.

In the Village, _____ can visit a _____ shop, a _____ hatchery, a _____ shop and a _____ to watch Acadians at work.

world	French	homes	New Brunswick	Caraquet	timbers
one	newspaper	eating	weave	loft	furniture
working	answer	spin	tinsmith's	prepare	lobster
fifty	buildings	tourists	sleeping	poor	cooper's
Acadie	greet				

Information

Kings Landing Historical Settlement

A New Brunswick Landmark

Kings Landing

Kings Landing Historical Settlement is located on the banks of the Saint John River in New Brunswick. It was created in 1960 when the Mactaquac Dam threathened to flood many historic buildings in the Saint John River Valley. This historical settlement is one of Canada's superior living museums interpreting society in the 19th century. Many loyal citizens left the American colonies during the American Revolution. They came to Canada because they wanted to remain loyal to the king of England and were known as United Empire Loyalists. The evolution of this society from its Loyalist roots to the Victorian era is reflected in the Kings Landing Historical Settlement.

Today, over 100 restored and reconstructed buildings and other structures are located at Kings Landing in a community setting. The collection of buildings includes homes and farmhouses, a sash and door factory, a gristmill, a sawmill, a general store, a parish school, several tradesmen's shops and a reconstructed sailing boat. Over 100 costumed interpreters go about rural life as it was in the province during the 19th century.

Visitors enjoy watching farmers caring for historic gardens and tending old-breed livestock. Antique farming equipment powered by horse and oxen may be met on the village roadways or seen in rail-fenced fields.

Costumed interpreters entertain visitors in the eleven historic homes with activities and tasks performed in early settler days such as spinning, weaving, sewing, baking bread, open hearth cooking and candle-making. Tradesmen such as the cooper, blacksmith, carpenter and miller demonstrate their skills. Tourists are often invited to help churn butter and spin flax or to chat to the blacksmith, the sawmill operator, the school teacher and the men running the ox cart. Delicious meals cooked using old recipes and early cooking methods may be enjoyed at the Kings Head Inn and the English-style pub.

Every day at Kings Landing is an exciting and informative window through which people may view a way of life experienced by the United Empire Loyalists.

Activity   Name: _____

Kings Landing Historical Settlement

A New Brunswick Landmark
Search and Find

In the word search:

colour the names of the buildings at Kings Landing **blue**.
colour the names of people working at Kings Landing **red**.

```
a h o u s e s l r w z c h u r c h i r j s k e
h m r w d e k q v z r s y t a q b p c o d f i
g c a r p e n t e r l u m v n w o c p x q a f
i n s x b g j m s x b k c j d i e o f h g r m
f i q v c f a r m h o u s e s w a o x z y m g
j o t y a h n o u y m r n s o t p p u q v e n
e k p u z f i p t a l b k c j d i e f h g r h
t d s c r b q a p z o y n x m w l r k v j u i
t g r i s t m i l l b v c w d x e y f z g a h
x i y j a z k a l b m c n d o e p f q g r h s
b m c n w d o e p f q g r h s i t j u k v l w
w a x b m y c z a g e n e r a l s t o r e z a
d u f u i h t j s l r n q r p s o t n v m y l
a e b g l c i d k e m f o g q h p i u j w k x
c s d n l e o f p g q h r i s j t k u l v m w
g c h i j k t l u m v n w o x p y q z r a s b
c h f d e s a s h a n d d o o r f a c t o r y
h o i b j a k z l m y m x n w o v p u q t r s
x o w y v z u a t b s c r d q p e o m f n g m
i l h g b l a c k s m i t h f e j d i c k b l
f q g r h s i t j u k v l w m x n y l o z p a
j e k d l c m b n a o z p y q x r w l s v t u
a i s c h o o l t e a c h e r b h c e d g e f
n r m i t f o g s h q i p j f k s l r m n o p
```

Information

The Hartland Covered Bridge

A New Brunswick Landmark

The **Hartland Covered Bridge** is located in a small community called Hartland in the province of New Brunswick. It is the longest covered bridge in the world measuring 390 metres in length and spans the Saint John River, one of the largest rivers in Canada. In 2001, the Hartland Covered Bridge celebrated its 100th birthday.

Early bridges were built out of timber from nearby forests. Wooden bridges were covered because the different types of weather caused the timbers to deteriorate. They also offered protection to travellers during storms and a place to rest.

The Hartland Covered Bridge

Citizens from communities on both sides of the Saint John River decided a bridge was needed to link the communities to increase trade and business. The citizens contributed money for its building. The bridge was built with wood and timbers from cedar, spruce and hard pine.

The bridge was to be completed on May 14, 1901 to be used by the people. An emergency call to a local doctor from a patient on the west side of the river forced the first person to cross the bridge twelve hours early. The doctor informed the workers about his circumstances at the bridge. Workers then placed planks so he could drive across it.

In 1906, the New Brunswick government purchased the bridge. Two spans of the bridge were taken out by ice on April 6, 1921. The government made major repairs and covered the bridge in 1922. A side walkway was added in 1947 for pedestrians to use.

On June 23, 1980, the Hartland Covered Bridge was declared a National Historic Site. Today, tourists from all over the world flock to see this famous covered bridge where sweethearts of days gone by stopped their horses and buggies to steal a kiss or two.

Activity

Name: _____

The Hartland Covered Bridge
A New Brunswick Landmark

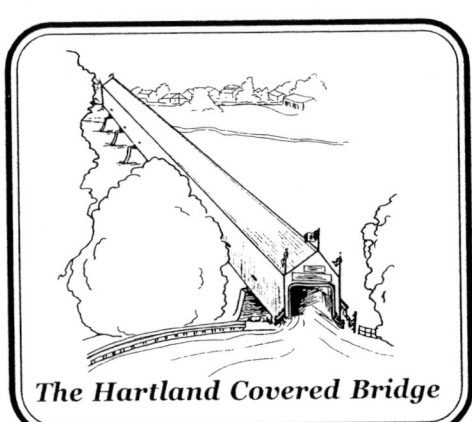
The Hartland Covered Bridge

The **Hartland Covered Bridge** is the longest covered bridge in the world.

How well did you **listen** to the discussion about it?

Join the beginnings and endings of the sentences below with a line to make them complete sentences about the Hartland Covered Bridge.

Beginnings	Endings
1. In 2001, the Hartland Covered Bridge	• the first citizen to cross the Bridge.
2. The Bridge spans	• gave money to build the Bridge.
3. The Hartland Covered Bridge is	• was one hundred years old.
4. It is the longest	• found in Hartland, New Brunswick.
5. The citizens from the two communities	• 390 metres long.
6. Wooden bridges were often covered to	• covered bridge in the world.
7. A local doctor was	• the Saint John River.
8. In 1980, the Hartland Covered Bridge	• protect them from all kinds of weather.
9. The Hartland Covered Bridge measures	• added so people could walk across the Bridge.
10. Later, a side walkway was	• was declared a National Historic Site.

© S&S Learning Materials

SSJ1-51

Information

Fundy Bay and the Hopewell Rocks

A New Brunswick Landmark

Hopewell Rocks

The **Bay of Fundy** is located between the provinces of New Brunswick and Nova Scotia. The Bay is 290 kilometres long. The mouth of the Bay is 100 kilometres wide and it is between 120 and 215 metres deep. This funnel-shaped bay gradually narrows until it splits to form Chignecto Bay and the Minas Basin. Chignecto Bay becomes gradually shallower and splits into Shepody Bay and Cumberland Basin. The Shepody Bay narrows and splits again into the Memramcook and Petitcodiac Rivers.

At the junction of the Memramcook and Petitcodiac Rivers, the **Hopewell Rocks** are found. Shepody Bay, at this point, is 2.5 kilometres wide and at low tide is about fourteen metres deep.

The Hopewell Rocks at Cape Hopewell, New Brunswick are one of the most popular tourist attractions in the province. This site is also the location of the highest tides in the world. For thousands of years, glaciers, fractures, and the incessant action of the Fundy Tides have hollowed out caves and pillars in the rocky cliffs to form the peculiar "flower pot rocks" (Hopewell Rocks). During low tide, the rocks and the beach around them may be explored. At high tide, the rocks form small islands. These fascinating natural sculptures provide homes for many animals who live in the grasses and trees that grow on the rocks.

During July for a six week period, two to three million shorebirds congregate in waves along several key locations in the upper reaches of Fundy Bay. It is their only stop on a 5 000 kilometre southbound journey from summer breeding grounds in the Arctic to their winter home along the southeast coast of South America, in the Guianas and Brazil. These birds are drawn to the Hopewell Rocks, Johnson's Mills and Mary's Point along the Bay of Fundy shoreline in New Brunswick because of a small amphipod, the mud shrimp, which lives in the salty mud. The mud shrimp burrows into the mud, then as the tide recedes, scurries to the surface to find mating burrows. On the mud flats there may be 10 000 to 20 000 tiny crustaceans in a square metre.

Flocks of shorebirds such as species of sandpipers and plovers may be seen feasting on these tasty treats. A single bird can eat 10 000 to 20 000 mud shrimp during a single tidal cycle. Each flock of birds stays in the area only long enough to double their weight to gain energy reserves for the remainder of their non-stop 4 000 kilometre flight over the ocean to South America.

During the shorebird migration, roosting areas such as the Hopewell Rocks are protected and visitors are requested to keep their distance to allow the birds to complete their mission undisturbed.

© S&S Learning Materials

Activity

Fundy Bay and the Hopewell Rocks

A New Brunswick Landmark

Hopewell Rocks

Many years ago, native Mikmaq knew the shores of the Bay of Fundy better than anyone. They told many colourful legends to explain the tides and the rock formations.

Read each Mikmaq legend carefully.

Choose **one** of the legends.

Illustrate the legend on a large sheet of paper.

Mikmaq Legends

The Tide

One day Glooscap, the great native god, decided to take a bath. Glooscap told Beaver to build a dam across the mouth of the bay to keep the high water in so he could bathe himself. Beaver did as he was told and built a dam.

Whale became angry. he wanted to know why the water had stopped flowing. Glooscap did not want to anger Whale so he told Beaver to go and break the dam. Whale did not want to wait that long. He began to break the dam apart with his great tail.

This caused the water to slosh back and forth with such force that it still does it today.

The Hopewell Rocks

Legend One

Many years ago, there were some poor Mikmaq who were slaves to angry whales who lived in the Bay. One day, some of the slaves decided to run away from the whales. They ran as far as the beach, but were then captured by the whales. The slaves were turned to stone. Their images today are encased in the stones called the Hopewell Rocks.

Legend Two

In the waters of the Bay lived a terrible monster. Everyone was afraid of it. The monster loved to eat white porpoises and to catch Mikmaq natives to make them its slaves.

One day, the monster was very hungry. He ordered his slaves to go fishing for the white porpoise. As soon as the slaves were out of the monster's sight, they began to run away. When the monster discovered the slaves were gone, he swung his tail up and down angrily. His tail churned up the water near the cliffs and carved the strange shapes we see in them today.

Information

Alexander Graham Bell National Historic Park

A Nova Scotia Landmark

Beinn Bhreagh

Alexander Graham Bell was born in Edinburgh, Scotland in 1847. In 1870, he came to Canada with his parents to live in Brantford, Ontario. One day in Brantford, the basic principle of the telephone came to him in a sudden flash of original insight. The first telephone was built in the United States and was tested between two rooms. On August 4, 1876, Bell sent a message from Mount Pleasant to Brantford, a distance of five miles.

All his life, Bell sought peace and strength in nature. He loved to spend time in the cool countryside where he could enjoy watching nature. Bell also found that his eyes were extremely sensitive to bright light. He often suffered from headaches brought on by stress and overwork.

Bell often took his family to the mountains or the seashore. On a holiday in 1885, he discovered the village of Baddeck. He fell in love with the village and the beautiful scenery which reminded him of Scotland but best of all, the weather was delightfully cool.

Bell and his wife decided to build a home to be called "Beinn Bhreagh" which means "beautiful mountain" in Gaelic. At first, the family lived in a thirteen-room house called "The Lodge" which was surrounded by gardens. A small playhouse called "Pansy Lodge" was built for the children.

Beinn Bhreagh was built on a point overlooking Baddeck. The large stone house was heated by eleven fireplaces. The largest stone fireplace was found in the main hall. Overlooking the Bras d'Or Lakes was a glassed-in-porch and stone terrace. The house was comfortably furnished to accommodate young people coming from the beach and sailing. Not far from the house was a tennis court and stone observatory that held Bell's telescope. There was also a boathouse that held a yacht called the "Elsie". On August 2, 1922, Alexander Graham Bell died at Baddeck, Nova Scotia. In respect for a life well-lived, the telephone service stopped for one minute on the time of his burial.

The artifacts and authentic records of his work were kept in the old kite house at Beinn Bhreagh, Bell's summer estate in Baddeck. 30 days after his death, his two daughters gave the contents of their father's old "museum" to the People of Canada. The Canadian government built a building to house this collection of artifacts. The Bell National Historic Site is located in Baddeck on his beloved shores of the Bras d'Or Lakes. The site contains the world's largest and most comprehensive collection of Bell's artifacts and archives. Replicas of early telephone models and over 600 poster-size photographs demonstrate the course of Bell's life.

Activity   Name: _____

Alexander Graham Bell Historic Park
A Nova Scotia Landmark

Beinn Bhreagh

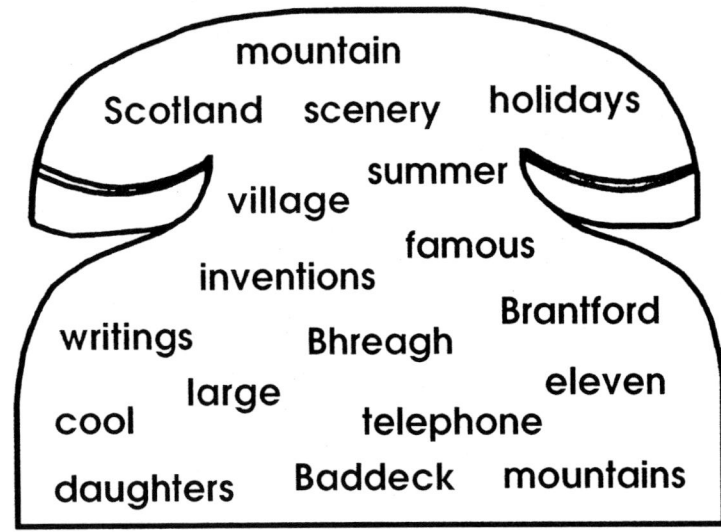

Use the words in the old telephone to **complete** the story about Alexander Graham Bell. **Print** the words on the lines provided.

Alexander Graham Bell came from _____ with his parents. They lived in _____, Ontario. Bell is a _____ man because he invented the _____.

He often took his family to the _____ or the seashore for _____. On one holiday, he visited a _____ in Nova Scotia called _____. He loved the beautiful _____ and the _____ weather. Bell and his wife decided to build a _____ home overlooking Baddeck. The house was called Beinn _____ which means "beautiful _____". It was a _____ house with _____ fireplaces.

After Alexander Graham Bell died, his _____ gave all of his _____ and _____ to the People of Canada.

The Canadian government built a large building to hold all of his artifacts in Baddeck.

© S&S Learning Materials   SSJ1-51

Information

Halifax Citadel National Historic Site

A Nova Scotia Landmark

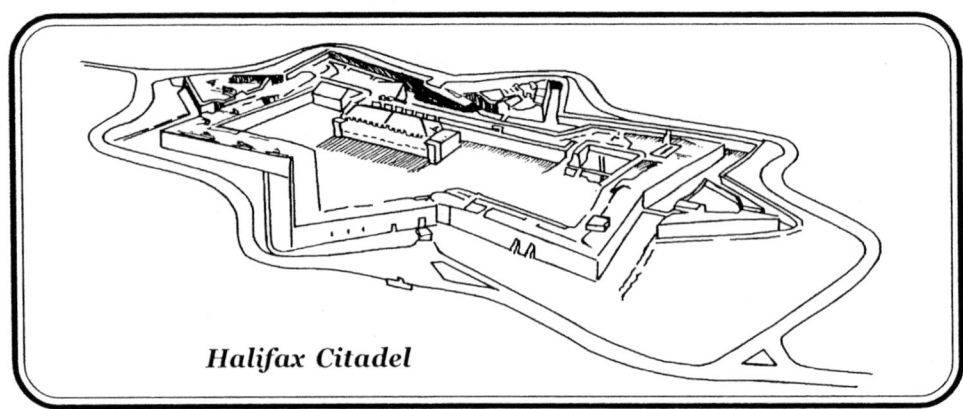
Halifax Citadel

High on a hill overlooking the harbour and downtown of Halifax, Nova Scotia sits the **Halifax Citadel National Historic Site.** In 1749, the British decided to build a great naval base at Halifax. It would be a permanent base for the Royal Navy operating in the Western Atlantic. Supplies would be stored here, naval ships would be repaired and it would provide a port for the province's trading needs. Halifax would also serve as the capital city of Nova Scotia. In three years, the town was home to 4 000 settlers, soldiers and sailors.

The Citadel or Fort was built by the British government to prevent the French navy from reaching the Gulf of St. Lawrence. Now the French settlers in New France and the Fortress of Louisbourg could be cut off from supplies of men and materials from France.

The Citadel, a star-shaped fort, was built on a green hill at the edge of Halifax's harbour. After the War of 1812, the city and its harbour was ringed with powerful batteries of cannon and thick stone ramparts. In the centre of Citadel Hill is the Citadel. It was dug deeply into the hill until it was almost invisible from the town. No enemy has ever attacked Citadel Hill.

Inside the Citadel, visitors will find a musket gallery, a powder magazine, garrison cells, a guard room, barracks for soldiers and a school room.

Costumed interpreters work at the Citadel to discuss the lifestyle and work as it was at the site during the late 1700s. Bagpipe music and marching soldiers may be enjoyed. Every day at noon, one of the cannons at the Citadel is fired to announce twelve o'clock. This is an old navy tradition still carried on today. People living and working in Halifax will often check their watches and clocks to make sure that they have the correct time.

In 1953, an Army Museum was established at the Citadel. The Museum has a collection of more than 70 000 artifacts. The focus of the Museum's display is a collection of artifacts that relate to the British, the Canadian Regular Force and other Military. These artifacts explain the roles of these units in the development of the British Empire and in the alliances of the Second World War.

Activity   Name: _____

Halifax Citadel National Historic Site

A Nova Scotia Landmark

Word list (in soldier's hat):
- cannon firing
- star-shaped
- navy ships
- supplies
- British
- Royal Navy
- French
- garrison cells
- bagpipe
- barracks

Each summer, the **Halifax Citadel** comes alive as soldiers parade, play their bagpipes and perform their drills.

How much did you learn about the Halifax Citadel?

Use the words in the soldier's hat to **answer** the questions. **Print** the words on the line provided under each one.

1. Who built the Halifax Citadel?
   _____

2. Who would be using the base?
   _____

3. What would be stored at the Citadel?
   _____

4. What would be repaired at the Citadel?
   _____

5. Who would not be able to get supplies and men to their forts?
   _____

6. In what shape did the British build the Citadel?
   _____

7. What kind of music will you hear at the Citadel?
   _____

8. Where did the soldiers live at the Citadel?
   _____

9. Where did they keep prisoners?
   _____

10. What do the citizens of Halifax still hear every day at noon?
    _____

© S&S Learning Materials   SSJ1-51

Information

Peggy's Cove

A Nova Scotia Landmark

Peggy's Cove

Peggy's Cove is a quaint fishing village nestled amongst gigantic granite rocks on the coast of Nova Scotia. It is said to be the most photographed fishing village in the world. There are various versions that tell how the Cove received its name. Some say that Peggy is the nickname for Margaret and the community may have acquired the name from nearby Saint Margaret's Bay, especially as the point marks the eastern entrance to the bay. Others feel Peggy was a settler that had lived there. Another version is a more romantic one. It tells about a woman named Peggy who was the sole survivor of a shipwreck in the area. She met and married one of the local men and spent the rest of her life in the village. Another story told is that a ship named Peggy sank nearby.

A marine artist who lived on Peggy's Cove believed the cove was named after the woman who survived the shipwreck. On the face of granite rock behind his house, he carved the images of 32 local fishermen, their wives and their children. He also included the image of the young woman of the shipwreck legend. This carving is known as the "Fisherman's Monument".

Despite all of the stories about its name, a lighthouse was built to mark the eastern entrance to St. Margaret's Bay in 1868. Although it is best known as the Peggy's Cove Lighthouse, its official name is "Peggy's Point Lighthouse" since its purpose was to mark the point not the cove. The first lighthouse was a wooden tower built above a lightkeeper's home. The light was red and it used a "catoptic reflector" (a round silver-plated mirror) to magnify the kerosene oil lamp.

In 1915, the wooden tower was replaced with a stout, concrete, octogan shaped tower approximately 15 metres west of the original light standing on large, smooth, wave-washed, granite rocks. These rocks are very dangerous to walk on and many tourists have lost their lives to the sea or have taken nasty falls.

The new lighthouse had a white light that came from a "dioptric lens", a series of glass prisms to magnify the light. In 1979, the colour of the light was changed from white to green. In 1969, the iron lantern on top of the tower was changed from white paint to red paint.

The Peggy's Point Lighthouse no longer serves as a beacon for navigational purposes. During summer months, it is used as the only fully operational post office in a lighthouse.

At Peggy's Cove there are many pleasant sights to see such as brightly painted buildings, the weathered fishing piers, the fishing boats tied to the docks, a restaurant, a gift shop and a post office.

On a bright sunny day, the Atlantic waters sparkle and shimmer in the sunlight. The sights, sounds and ocean smells excite the avid photographer and painter.

Activity

Name: _____

Peggy's Cove
A Nova Scotia Landmark

Peggy's Cove is one of Canada's famous places that people like to visit, photograph and paint.

Use the words in the lighthouse to complete the sentences about Peggy's Cove.

Print the words on the lines provided.

red
carved
tower
keeper
second
warn
concrete
granite
stories
white
colour
post office
wood
lamp
green
fishing
lantern
name
point

1. Peggy's Cove is a _____ village in Nova Scotia.
2. An artist _____ pictures of the village people on a big _____ rock.
3. The first lighthouse was a _____ made out of _____.
4. A lighthouse _____ looked after the first light.
5. The first light was a kerosene oil _____.
6. The _____ lighthouse was made out of _____ and stands on smooth granite rocks.
7. There are many _____ told about how Peggy's Cove got its _____.
8. At first, the _____ of the light in the second lighthouse was _____ but was later turned to _____.
9. The Peggy's _____ Lighthouse is no longer used to _____ boats of danger, but is used as a _____ during the summer.
10. The iron _____ at the top of the lighthouse was changed from white paint to _____ paint.

© S&S Learning Materials

SSJ1-51

Information

Montmorency Falls Park

A Quebec Landmark

Montmorency Falls

A short distance, east of the city of Quebec, a beautiful wonder of nature is found in Montmorency Park. The park is the home to **Montmorency Falls** which is 83 metres tall (30 metres higher than Niagara Falls).

The explorer Samuel de Champlain discovered and named the falls "The Sault de Montmorency" after the Viceroy of New France, Admiral Henry de Montmorency. The land on either side of the falls was given to a Frenchman who supported the King of France. The land was passed from person to person until 1759 when General James Wolfe led his English troups to capture Quebec City. In order to do this, he had to cross the river of Montmorency Falls. His men found this difficult and after a short and bloody battle, Wolfe retreated leaving 200 of his men dead on the battlefield. Quebec was safe for a while. England was determined to make New America a British colony, and their wish came true when Wolfe and his British soldiers defeated Montcalm and his men on the Plains of Abraham.

In 1778, Sir Frederick Haldimand became a governor of the British Province of Quebec. He built a beautiful villa at the rim of the falls. Many gala balls and social events took place in this charming villa by the falls. In 1790, the villa was rented by Prince Edward Augustus, the son of King George III. He was a rather unpopular member of the family and was sent to Quebec to command the 7th Regiment of his Majesty's forces. Prince Edward felt very lonely and rejected by his family, so he sent a messenger to France that year to find a young lady to keep him company. Theresa-Bernadine Mangenet came to Canada and spent 27 years with him. In time, they became a beloved and cherished couple in this French speaking land.

In 1818, his father ordered him to return to England to marry, by arrangement, a German princess, in order to give an heir to the throne. In 1819, he became a father to a girl, and a year later he died. His daughter grew up to become Queen Victoria.

Today, the great villa beside the falls has become an inn named Manoir Montmorency. The inn has a restaurant, reception rooms and boutiques. Tourists may travel up to it by a cable car, or they may climb the 487 stairway of steps and then cross two suspension bridges that span the falls.

There has always been a bridge over the Falls but not all were safe to use. On April 30, 1856, five days after it was opened, the suspension bridge collapsed, sending a farmer, his wife and a friend to their deaths in the water below.

Activity   Name: _____

Montmorency Falls Park
A Quebec Landmark

Montmorency Falls Park is a beautiful place to visit while you are travelling in Quebec.

How well can you recall facts you have learned?

Answer each question with word(s) found in the cable car.

Print the answer on the line provided at the end of each question.

487 steps
Niagara Falls   lonely
Queen Victoria   83 metres
a beautiful villa an inn
to get married   a cable car
Samuel de Champlain

1. What is the name of the man who named Montmorency Falls?
   _____

2. How high is Montmorency Falls?
   _____

3. What is the name of the famous falls that is lower than Montmorency Falls?
   _____

4. What did Prince Edward, the English Governor, build near Montmorency Falls?
   _____

5. How did Prince Edward feel during his stay in Quebec?
   _____

6. Why did Prince Edward return to England?
   _____

7. What is the name of his daughter?
   _____

8. What is the great villa today?
   _____

9. What carries people up to the inn?
   _____

10. How many steps lead up to the inn?
    _____

© S&S Learning Materials   31   SSJ1-51

Information

Quebec City

A Quebec Landmark

Chateau Frontenac

Quebec City is the capital city of the province of Quebec. It stands guard over the St. Lawrence River and is the only walled city on the continent north of Mexico.

Samuel de Champlain, a French explorer, established a settlement where Quebec City stands today, called the "Habitation of Quebec". Champlain and his men built a cluster of buildings by the river's edge. During their first winter, most of the pioneers of Quebec died of the cold, scurvy and lack of food.

In 1985, the United Nations declared Old Quebec a World Heritage Site. It is the oldest city in North America with magnificent views, charming squares and some of the oldest buildings. Steep-roofed stone houses, restaurants and outdoor cafes line the narrow streets that wind through the heart of the old city.

The old city is made up of two areas - "Upper Town", perched on top of Cape Diamant, and "Lower Town" below on the bank of the St. Lawrence River.

In the centre of Upper Town is a square called "Place d'Armes" which was a drill and parade ground many years ago. Near the square can be found the "Citadel", a star-shaped fortress that took 30 years to build during the mid 1800s. The Citadel was built to withstand a repeat attack on the city from across the Plains of Abraham to the southwest. At the Citadel, tourists can view 25 buildings, including the "Cape Diamond Redoubt" (an old fortress) of 1693, the Governor General's residence and five heavily fortified bastions (parts of a fortification that stick out so that the defenders can fire at attackers from as many angles as possible). At the regimental museum, which was a former powderhouse, visitors can view firearms, uniforms, insignia and other items from the 17th century onwards.

The Citadel is the home of the "Van Doos" (Vingt-deux), the "Royal 22nd Regiment", the prestigious French-speaking regiment of the Canadian Forces. In the summer, two ceremonies are held - the "Changing of the Guard" and "The Retreat". During the Changing of the Guard, the Regimental Band plays while the men march and perform their duties accompanied by the Citadel's mascot - "Batisse", a goat, who is also the regiment's mascot. In the evening, the Royal 22nd Regiment performs "The Retreat" as part of the flag-lowering ceremonies.

Just south of the Citadel is 101 hectares of rolling parkland known as the "Plains of Abraham". On this site, the famous fifteen minute battle that led to the end of the French regime in Quebec took place. In the early morning of September 13, 1759, standing in the drizzling rain, the British troops of **General Wolfe** were ready to resist the defending French troops under **General Montcalm**. Wolfe and his men made their way up from the St. Lawrence River with great stealth and easily overcame the sleeping French soldiers at the top of the cliff. Montcalm and his men were taken by surprise; they advanced in disorder and were cut to pieces by the redcoats' sustained fire. Wolfe perished on the battlefield and Montcalm died from his wounds the following day. The events that took place on this day changed the course of Canada's future.

In "Upper Town", towering above Quebec City is the "Chateau Frontenac Hotel". It is owned by the Canadian Pacific Hotels and Resorts. This huge Victorian building, with its gables and turrets and green copper rooves was built in 1893 on top of Cape Diamond high above the river. It has more than 600 guest rooms and many famous people have met here for conferences.

"Lower Town" can be reached by walking down the "Casse-Cou" (breakneck) stairway or by taking the funicular (a type of train). A square called Place Royale, is the site of the early French Settlement. It has old restored buildings, artists' workshops and boutiques.

Activity

Quebec City

A Quebec Landmark

Chateau Frontenac

Quebec City is an interesting city filled with old houses, narrow streets, squares, a fort and beautiful parks.

Read the sentences about Quebec City carefully.

Put a **check mark** in the box beside each sentence about Quebec City.

☐ Quebec City is the oldest city in the world.

☐ In Upper Town, there is a fort called the Citadel.

☐ Old Quebec City is made of Upper Town and Lower Town.

☐ Most of the buildings in Quebec City are modern stores, houses and restaurants.

☐ Upper Town and Lower Town have a stone wall with gates around them.

☐ The Chateau Frontenac is a huge church that sits high above the city.

☐ On the Plains of Abraham, a big battle took place between the French and the English.

☐ Lower Town is the place where the early settlers lived.

☐ The English won the battle that took place on the Plains of Abraham.

☐ Quebec City is the capital city of Ontario.

☐ The Citadel is a star-shaped fortress found in Lower Town.

☐ The Van Doos are a French-speaking regiment of the Canadian Military and make the Citadel their base.

Information

Percé Rock

A Quebec Landmark

Percé Rock

The **Gaspé Peninsula** is one of the oldest land masses on the earth. It is located in the province of Quebec. Its interior is covered with a vast, mainly uninhabited, forest and the Chic Choc Mountains. Sheer cliffs, worn away by the water and wind, are seen along the coastline. Visitors travel through tiny coastal fishing communities with unusual names that appear to cling to the shoreline. The Micmaq Native People have lived in the Gaspé Peninsula for over 2 500 years. The name Gaspé probably comes from a Micmaq word meaning "land's end".

Vikings, Basques and Portuguese fishermen explored the area long before Jacques Cartier landed on the Gaspé in 1534, although settlers did not start to arrive until the late 18th century. The Acadians came to this area in 1755 and founded the communities of Bonaventure and Carleton after being displaced by the British from New Brunswick. Many of the early settlers were loyalists and were loyal to the King of England who fled the United States after the American Revolution.

One of the most famous sites in the Gaspé Peninsula is the huge black rock off the shore of the town of Percé. The **Percé Rock** dominates the village and is quite a tourist attraction. At low tide people walk out to the rock to view it. The Rock is 438 metres long, 100 metres wide, 88 metres high and weighs five trillion tonnes. It is 375 million years old.

The name "Percé" was given to the rock because the ocean "pierced" holes in it to form huge archways. At one time, there were two holes or archways but today there is only one large one that is about 30 metres wide. Percé Rock is full of thousands of fossils. Tour boats take people around the rock and to Bonaventure Island. People are usually impressed with the size, colour and beauty of the rock.

Bonaventure Island is a nesting place for seabirds. Over 200 thousand birds are found on the wind swept island each year, including the largest colony of gannets. Other seabirds are puffins, comorants and murres. Tourists are amazed with the number of seabirds on the island.

Activity Name: _____

Percé Rock

A Quebec Landmark

Percé Rock is a huge piece of limestone rock sitting in the Atlantic Ocean.

Complete the paragraph about Percé Rock with the words found in the rowboat.

Print the words on the lines provided.

Percé Rock

Percé _____ is very famous. People come to _____ it every year. They are surprised with its _____, colour and how _____ it looks. Percé Rock is 438 metres _____, 100 metres _____ and 88 metres _____. It _____ five trillion tonnes and is 375 _____ years old. There is a large _____ in the rock made by the _____. Percé Rock is full of _____. When the tide is out, people can _____ out to see it.

hole   long
ocean   weighs   high   size
wide   Rock   beautiful
fossils million   visit   walk

Information

Niagara Falls

An Ontario Landmark

Niagara Falls

Niagara Falls is located on the Niagara River about half way between Lake Erie and Lake Ontario. The Niagara River forms part of the border between Canada and the United States.

Niagara Falls is made of two waterfalls, the "Horseshoe Falls" on the Canadian side of the border and the "American Falls" on the United States side. The Horseshoe Falls is in the province of Ontario and the American Falls in the state of New York.

The Niagara River plunges into a steep gorge at the falls. The Niagara Gorge extends for about eleven kilometres to Lewiston, New York. About five kilometres below the Falls the famous Whirlpool Rapids begin.

The Horseshoe Falls is about 51 metres high and 792 metres wide at its widest point. The American Falls is about 54 metres high and 305 metres wide.

The Niagara Gorge is about 61 metres deep and is made of layers of different kinds of stone. Dolomite, a hard rock, about 24 metres thick forms the top layer. Softer layers of dolomite, limestone, sandstone and shale lie underneath. Water erodes soft stone faster than hard stone and for this reason, the top layer extends beyond the lower layers in many places. Behind the American Falls, a cave named the "Cave of the Winds", has been formed under an extended shelf of harder stone.

The Niagara Gorge has become longer and longer over the years. The pounding water has eroded the soft rock causing the unsupported hard rock ledge to collapse. The ledge of the Horseshoe Falls is wearing away faster than the ledge of the American Falls because more water pours over it.

Niagara Falls attracts visitors from all over the world each year. Several steamers called the "Maid of the Mist" take tourists close to the churning waters at the base of the falls. Canada and the United States use the water of the Niagara Falls to produce electricity.

Maid of the Mist — Maid of the Mist IV

Niagara Falls

An Ontario Landmark

Niagara Falls is a popular tourist attraction, and visited by people from all over the world.

Choose words from the box that will complete the story about Niagara Falls. **Print** the words on the lines provided.

Niagara Falls is found on the _____ River between Lake _____ and Lake _____.

The _____ Falls is on the Canadian side while the _____ Falls is on the American side of the river.

Niagara Falls _____ many visitors each year. Several _____ called _____ takes tourists close to the _____ waters at the base of the falls. Both Canada and the United States use the _____ of Niagara Falls to produce _____.

There are many _____ in Niagara Falls. One of the more well-known is the Criminals Hall of Fame Wax Museum. Also in Niagara Falls are Historic Fort Erie and the Laura Secord Homestead.

Niagara Falls is also the home of many other amusements including the African Lion Safari and _____. Here you can come to see _____, _____ and many other water creatures along with deer and other animals.

Ontario	Horseshoe	Niagara	American	museums
attracts	Erie	churning	electricity	whales
steamers	water	Maid of the Mist	Marineland	seals

Information

Niagara Falls

An Ontario Landmark

The Niagara Falls Legend

Seneca girl paddling her canoe to the edge of Niagara Falls

A long time ago, a beautiful girl from a Seneca tribe was told by her father that she would have to marry an old and ugly man. She was so upset that she planned a way to escape. One day, the girl jumped into her canoe and pushed off into the fast flowing Niagara River. She felt it was better to die in the river's angry waters than to marry a man that she hated.

In a cave, behind the rushing waters of the Niagara River, lived the great chief of the clouds, rain and of the harvest named Thunderer. He noticed the girl's canoe floating to the edge of the falls and saw her unhappy face. In a few minutes her boat would be smashed against the rocks below. Quickly, he spread his wings and flew to save her. Thunderer caught her just before her boat crashed into pieces.

The native girl lived with Thunderer in his cave for a long time. Thunderer taught her many things. The girl learned that a snake monster lived under the ground beneath her village. The snake monster came out to poison their drinking water because he liked to eat people.

Thunderer told the girl that her people would have to move their village closer to the lake. When the ugly old man died, Thunderer told the girl she could return to her village and to tell her people all about the things she had been taught.

When the village people heard the girl's news, they broke up their homes and moved the village closer to the lake. For a while, all was well in the village.

In time, the village people began to die from the fever-sickness again. The snake monster had returned. He hoped to kill as many people in the new village as he had in the old village. One night, Thunderer saw him creeping along the ground. As the snake monster neared the village, he threw thunderbolts at him and killed him.

The dead snake monster was very large. When the people stretched it out they found it to be longer than twenty arrow-flights. The snake monster was pushed into the waters of the Niagara River and the village people watched it float to the narrow part. They were afraid the snake monster would not get through the narrow place between the rocks.

When the snake monster reached the narrows, it could not go any further. It was caught between the rocks. The water of the river was forced to rise above the snake monster and then fell in a giant cascade. The weight of the snake monster pressed on the rocks, pushed them back and bent them into the shape of a giant bow.

The village people never had the fever-sickness again. The giant waterfall, in the shape of a great hunting bow that is bent, stays in the Niagara River to remind the native people of their friend and protector, the Thunderer.

Activity

Niagara Falls

An Ontario Landmark

Listen to the story called "The Niagara Falls Legend".

Answer each question with a **complete** sentence.

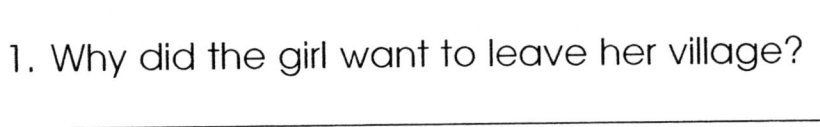

Seneca Girl in boat

1. Why did the girl want to leave her village?

2. How did the girl plan to escape?

3. Why did Thunderer save the girl?

4. What was making the people in the village sick?

5. Why did the people move their village?

6. How was Niagara Falls formed?

7. In the box below, illustrate your favourite part of the Seneca legend.

Information

Ste. Marie Among the Hurons

An Ontario Landmark

The area between Georgian Bay and Lake Simcoe is known as "Huronia", the land of the Hurons. This is one of Ontario's most historic areas. In an area close to where the present town of Midland now stands, a group of Jesuit priests set out to convert the Huron Native People to Christianity.

Jean de Brébuf and a group of priests were the first missionaries to contact the Hurons. In 1634, they travelled nearly 500 kilometres from Quebec to the shores of Georgian Bay. It took them almost a month to get there. The Hurons called the priests "black robes" and showed little interest in what they were doing. The priests lived in Huron longhouses and ate Huron food. They learned the Huron language and how to hunt for food. After being with the Huron people for five years, the priests decided to build a permanent mission. They called it **Ste. Marie**.

The Jesuit priests built a bakery and shops for blacksmiths, carpenters and shoemakers. A dormitory and a chapel was built for the priests and a hospital and chapel for the Hurons. The Jesuits planted crops and brought in livestock. 66 Jesuits and workers lived in Ste. Marie at one time.

The Ste. Marie mission existed for only ten years. The Iroquois, a neighbouring tribe, had been making attacks on Huronia. The Jesuits tried to help settle the struggle for control of the fur trade, but they were not successful. The smaller missions and Huron villages throughout Huronia were destroyed. Many settlements were burned and people living in them were killed or taken prisoner and tortured. Fathers Brébuf, Garnier, Lalement, Daniel and Chabanel were tortured until they died. The only settlement that remained was Ste. Marie.

The priests and the Hurons did not want the Iroquois to capture the mission so they decided to burn it down. They packed their belongings and supplies into their canoes and then set fire to the mission. As they slowly paddled from the shore, they turned to watch the buildings and surrounding wall burn to the ground.

Today, Ste. Marie Among the Hurons has been reconstructed as a living museum. It has 22 reproduced structures including a longhouse, and a wigwam. Costumed interpreters go about performing their 17th century tasks while they answer visitors' questions. Fires burn in the great stone fireplaces once again and the gardens have been replanted. Ste. Marie Among the Hurons is a place where people can experience what it was like for the first European visitors living among the Hurons.

Near the Ste. Marie settlement is the Midland Shrine which is dedicated to the six priests who were tortured to death by the Iroquois.

© S&S Learning Materials

Activity

Ste. Marie Among the Hurons

An Ontario Landmark

Ste. Marie Among the Hurons is a mission built by French priests close to the town of Midland.

Complete the story with words from the Huron pot.

Print the words on the lines provided.

Read the story to find out why Ste. Marie Among the Hurons is an important place.

Words in the pot: destroy, war, killed, God, tortured, priests, chapel, Hurons, ten, bakery, attacked, corn, fish, hospital, mission, burn, wilderness, Ste. Marie

A group of French _____ travelled to the land of the _____. They wanted to teach the native people about _____ and to help them. They built a _____ and called it _____. The mission had a _____, a blacksmith's shop, a carpenter's shop and a dormitory for the priests, a _____ and a _____.

The Hurons taught the French priests how to live in the _____. They also brought them _____ and dried _____.

The mission only lasted for _____ years. The Iroquois had declared _____ on the Huron nation. Many smaller missions and Huron villages were _____ and destroyed. People were _____ and _____.

The priests and Hurons at Ste. Marie decided to _____ down the mission before they left so the Iroquois couldn't _____ it.

Information

The CN Tower

An Ontario Landmark

The CN Tower

The **CN Tower** is almost twice as tall as the Eiffel Tower in France and more than three times the height of the Washington Monument. It dominantes the Toronto skyline proudly. It was built by the Canadian National Railway or CNR, as a transmission tower to improve signals delivered to televisions in Toronto homes.

Work on the foundation began in 1973 with giant backhoes excavating 56 000 metric tonnes of earth and shale to a depth of fifteen metres.

Pre-stressed concrete and reinforced steel were arranged in a Y-shaped pattern 6.6 metres thick. Each hollow leg of the Y would carry its fair share of the tower's 181.8 metric tonne burden. The foundation took four months to complete.

The next section of the tower was made from a huge mould called a "slip-form" that moved upward as the poured concrete hardened. The mould gradually decreased in width giving the tower its shape. At the 330 metre mark, the builders prepared to build the "Sky Pod", a seven-storey structure housing two observation decks, a revolving restaurant, a nightclub and broadcasting equipment. The Sky Pod is reached by four high-speed, glass-fronted elevators whose rapid rise provides visitors with a very thrilling ride.

Above the Sky Pod is found the "Space Deck", 488 metres up. Breathtaking views from the glass-enclosed balcony may be viewed by visitors. On a good day, sites that are 120 kilometres away may be seen.

For the last phase of the tower, a Sikorsky Skycrane helicopter installed the tower's 165.5 metre communication mast. One by one, the helicopter lifted about 40 seven-tonne sections of the mast to the top of the tower, where workers braved blustery March winds to receive them. The sections were held in place with 40 000 bolts. The completed mast was then encased in a fibreglass reinforced sheath to prevent icing.

The CN Tower was completed in 1975 costing 57 million dollars. It became the tallest free-standing structure in the world.

Since then, the tower has gained two new elevators to accommodate the increase in visitors. The elevators take off like rockets achieving an ascent of six metres a second, about the same as a jet plane taking off. Walking down the 2 579 steps takes about twenty minutes. No one cares to walk to the top by the stairs. The metal staircase was moved from the outside of the Tower to the inside to accommodate the elevators. A glass floor was added to the Sky Pod's observation deck. Brave visitors, the majority children, inch out over the visual void. The experience is awesome from the top of the 544.7 metre landmark.

Activity

Name: _____

The CN Tower

An Ontario Landmark

The **CN Tower** is a famous Canadian landmark and is visited by thousands of visitors from all over the world each year.

How much do you remember about the CN Tower?

Read each sentence carefully.

Print **True** or **False** on the line at the end of each one.

1. The CN Tower is 2 000 metres high. _____
2. The Tower was built of concrete and steel. _____
3. A large car company built the CN Tower in 1973. _____
4. The glass-fronted elevators carry people slowly to the Observation Deck. _____
5. The Sky Pod is seven storeys high. _____
6. There are 2 597 stone spiral steps leading to the top of the CN Tower. _____
7. The Sky Pod has a revolving restaurant and two observation decks with glass floors. _____
8. The CN Tower is the tallest free-standing structure in the world. _____
9. It is always foggy at the top of the Tower. _____
10. A Skycrane helicopter was used to put the last seven sections on the tower. _____
11. The CN Tower and the Eiffel Tower in France are the same height. _____
12. The CN Tower was built to improve the picture on televisions in Toronto homes. _____
13. It is faster to walk up the 2 579 steps to the Space Deck than it is to take the elevators. _____
14. On a good day, people can view beautiful scenery that is 120 kilometres away. _____

© S&S Learning Materials

Information

Mennonite Heritage Village

A Manitoba Landmark

Mennonite Windmill

Between 1874 and 1879, almost 18 000 **Mennonites** left Russia for Canada. Entire villages were taken from the Russian steppes to the province of Manitoba. The Mennonites came to Canada looking for the freedom to practise their own faith and to educate their children in their church-run schools.

The Mennonites believe in leading productive lives. They are hard working and industrious. Work to a Mennonite is about more than a paycheck. They feel work keeps the mind and body well, gives one a meaningful activity, and a way to help society.

Mennonites are pacifists and they are exempt from military service. They lead a simple lifestyle and they believe one should never take oneself too seriously. They dress in a simple style, live in simple homes and attend modest and plainly decorated churches.

In Steinbach, Manitoba, there is a **Mennonite Heritage Village** which brings to life a way of life from the 14th centuty to present day. The Village is located on a 17 hectare site that spreads out from a village street in a pattern similar to Mennonite villages found throughout Southern Manitoba at the turn of the century. The north side of the street shows the early settlement buildings. The south side has the various businesses.

There are many types of buildings in the village. The "Semlin" are crude buildings made from sod, soil, grass and wood. These were the first buildings lived in by the Mennonites on the Manitoba prairies. There is a log house and a Mennonite House-Barn. A separate building called a summer kitchen was used during the hot summer months to prepare family meals so that the large house would remain cool. A clay outdoor oven was once used to bake delicious breads and buns. Straw is used to make a fire hot enough to bake two batches of bread at a time. The church is located in the centre of the village. The sails of the windmill turn in the wind as the wheat is ground into flour. A blacksmith shop displays a forge and tools used by a blacksmith to perform a wide variety of jobs. The public school is a typical one-room rural school. The printery is a typical western Canadian print shop complete with drawers of handset type and a Platen Press. At the general store, old fashioned stick candy, handicrafts, seeds and toys may be purchased. These are just a few of the many buildings found at the Mennonite Heritage Village. Other Mennonite activities such as quilting, cooking, baking, storytelling, spinning and weaving take place as well in the village.

Activity Name: _____

Mennonite Heritage Village
A Manitoba Landmark

Mennonite Windmill

The **Mennonite Heritage Village** shows the simple way of life led by Mennonites many years ago.

In the **Village** are different buildings used by the early Mennonites.

Match the name of a building to each sentence. **Print** its name on the line provided.

church	blacksmith shop	public school
printery	summer kitchen	general store
windmill	log house	farm barns and pens
semlin		

1. Sod, soil, grass and wood were used to build this kind of house.
   _____

2. Meals were cooked here during the hot summers.
   _____

3. It had oak log walls, a thatched roof and several rooms.
   _____

4. This building was in the centre of town and was used on Sunday.
   _____

5. It was a one-room building used by Mennonite children.
   _____

6. The Mennonites had metal things that were made in this building.
   _____

7. Mennonites could buy supplies that they needed in this building.
   _____

8. Farm animals and their families were kept here in the summer.
   _____

9. This shop has a printing press and handset type.
   _____

10. This building is an amazing structure that ground wheat into flour.
    _____

© S&S Learning Materials

Information

York Factory National Historic Site
A Manitoba Landmark

York Factory

York Factory is located near the mouth of the Hayes River approximately 250 kilometres south-east of Churchill, Manitoba. This site was chosen by the Hudson's Bay Company as it was accessible by ocean-going boats and provided a safe harbour. Supplies and goods were transferred to York Factory and then transported by smaller boats that travelled on smaller, navigable rivers to small inland communities. The establishment of York Factory provided the Hudson Bay Company with access to good quality furs and native trading.

The 171 year old Hudson's Bay Company Depot at York Factory is the oldest and largest wooden building in Canada. It stands on permanently frozen ground known as permafrost. The building is very important to Canadian History. The story about the lives of the employees and their work is told in the artifacts and the remains of the building from the 18th and 19th centuries. The site is comprised of 102 hectares of land on which the Hudson's Bay Company's Depot building stands.

There have been three forts on this site. The first fort had a brick and stone foundation and brick and wood walls. This type of building worked well in England but was not flexible enough for the heaving and pressure of the Canadian permafrost. The building quickly fell apart and could no longer be used.

The current site, known as York Factory III was developed after 1788. In 1850, the post lost its importance and was abandoned by the Hudson's Bay Company in 1957. In 1968, the post was given to the Government of Canada.

Activity

York Factory National Historic Site

A Manitoba Landmark

York Factory was a very important fur trading post for 250 years.

Complete the story about York Factory with the words found in the box.

Print the words on the lines provided.

Read the story to a friend.

York Factory is found on the Hayes _____ in the province of _____. It belonged to the Hudson's Bay Company. It was a _____ post where people traded _____ for goods.

The Hudson's Bay Company Depot at York Factory is 171 _____ old. It is the _____ wooden building in Canada. The Depot stands on permanently _____ ground called _____.

There have been _____ posts on this site. The first two _____ and _____ buildings could not take the _____ and _____ of the permafrost.

pressure	River	heaving	Manitoba	trading
brick	oldest	frozen	years	furs
permafrost	three	stone		

Information

The Big Muddy Badlands

A Saskatchewan Landmark

Castle Butte

The **Big Muddy Badlands** region is located just north of the international boundary separating south-central Sasaktchewan from northeastern Montana. In the Badlands is the **Big Muddy Valley.** It is 55 kilometres long, 3 kilometres wide and 160 metres deep.

The hills in the "Big Muddy" are smooth, rounded, and rolling, and covered with natural grass. Other land formations are buttes, cliffs and hogbacks that reveal layers of sedimentary rock. A "butte" is a steep, flat-topped hill that stands alone. A "hogback" is a low, sharp ridge with steep sides.

Castle Butte is a 70 metre high sandstone and clay formation. It sits in a prominent position on the flat valley floor. It was a landmark used for navigation by the Native tribes, early surveyors, the North-West Mounted Police patrols, outlaws and settlers. There are pathways that lead to the top and may be used in good weather.

Throughout the Big Muddy Badlands are found teepee rings, cairns (a pile of stones heaped up as a memorial, tomb or landmark), and other ceremonial boulder arrangements. The area was popular with Native Peoples for several thousand years. It is here that they once hunted the buffalo. Mule deer, antelope, white-tailed deer, coyotes, red fox, badgers, weasels, skunks and porcupines make their homes in the Badlands. Numerous birds of prey thrive in the Badlands such as golden eagles, prairie falcons and hawks.

Although the climate is dry in the Badlands, a diverse variety of plants are able to grow. In spring, the Big Muddy is quite colourful when the cactus and wildflowers are in bloom.

The Big Muddy Badlands was at one time a haven for notorious outlaws such as Butch Cassidy, Sam Kelley and Dutch Henry. The Big Muddy was known as Station Number One on an Outlaw Trail that began in this ruggedly serene valley in Saskatchewan. The trail went through the American states of Montana, Colorado and Arizona into Mexico. Butch Cassidy, a famous outlaw, organized the trail. Along the trail were ranches with fresh horses every ten to twelve kilometres along the way. Lawmen pursuing Cassidy and his Wild Bunch gang were almost always left in the dust. Outlaws travelled back and forth across the border frequently. The harsh geography of the Big Muddy made the Mounties' task of patrolling the area very difficult.

Activity

The Big Muddy Badlands

A Saskatchewan Landmark

Castle Butte

The **Big Muddy Badlands** was once a favourite spot used as a hideout by outlaws and cattle rustlers many years ago.

Complete the story about the Badlands with words from the cowboy boot.

Print the words on the lines provided.

The Big Muddy Badlands is found in southern _____ near the Canada and United States _____. In the Badlands is a large, deep _____ called the Big _____ Valley that is 55 kilometres long. The _____ in the Badlands are _____, rounded and rolling, and they are covered in _____. Other land forms are _____, _____, and _____.

A butte is a _____, flat-topped hill that stands _____ in the valley. _____ Butte is one.

In the Big Muddy Badlands, Native People once _____ and _____ the buffalo. Today, mule _____, antelope, white-tailed deer, _____, _____, badgers, _____, skunks and porcupines live in this area. Golden _____, prairie _____ and _____ swoop about hunting for food. In the spring, the Badlands are coloured with blooming _____ and _____.

border
lived
cliffs
hunted
valley
coyotes
steep
eagles
Muddy
falcons
ridges
hills
hawks
smooth
cactus
deer
buttes
grass
foxes
wildflowers
Saskatchewan
alone
Castle
weasels

Information

World's Largest Tomahawk

A Saskatchewan Landmark

Poundmaker, chief of the Plains Cree, led his band of warriors into the town of Battleford, Saskatchewan. The band was in need of food and farming tools. The settlers of Battleford were terrified of Poundmaker and his band because they had heard of native people killing settlers in other neighbouring areas. The settlers barricaded themselves inside the Northwest Mounted Police Fort. Poundmaker asked the Native Agent to get the supplies they needed. The Native Agent was afraid to come out and refused to see him. The men in the band became very angry and looted the town's Hudson Bay Company store and some settlers' homes.

The Natives knew that Canadian troops were in the area and they would retaliate. Poundmaker and his warriors set up a war lodge. War Chief Fine Day became the leader of the band. Fine Day moved the Cree camp to Cut Knife Hill.

Lieutenant-Colonel Otter planned to move under the cover of night to attack the Natives on the morning of May 2, 1885, at dawn. Poundmaker and his warriors were ready for the attack because a Native village never sleeps.

The government troops took up position on the high Cut Knife Hill overlooking the Native camp. From the hill, they could fire their cannons down on the teepees of the Cree. The Natives hid in the wooded valleys below. It suited their way of fighting. Although their guns were old, the Native warriors were good marksmen. Snipers were able to pick off Colonel Otter's troops one by one. Gradually, the Cree crept through the brush and encircled the base of the hill surrounding Otter and his troops. The troops were using a "Gatling Gun" (an early machine gun) and the noise of its rattle frightened the Natives at first. They soon realized the bullets were whizzing over their heads harmlessly. Two of the troops' cannons refused to fire and by late morning, Colonel Otter knew he was in serious trouble. The amount of wounded soldiers was growing rapidly in number. The Native war cries were coming closer. Colonel Otter knew that the Cree would soon surround him and cut off his only line of retreat across Cut Knife Creek. Otter gave the order to retreat.

The Cree wanted to pursue the fleeing soldiers, but Poundmaker told them it is acceptable to defend their women and children but not to go on the attack. If Poundmaker had not stopped the warriors, Otter's retreat would have turned into a disaster because the troops wouldn't have been able to defend themselves as they forded Cut Knife Creek.

Cut Knife is a small community found west of Battleford, Saskatchewan. The population of Cut Knife is nearly 600. The people living in the area are descendents of settlers from the British Isles, Italy, the Ukraine, Scandinavia and the Plains Cree. The immigrants settled the Cut Knife district in the 1900s. Today, it is a prosperous farming area and community.

On the west side of Cut Knife, in Tomahawk Park, is the **World's Largest Tomahawk**. The Tomahawk is a symbol of unity and friendship between the First nations and the white population in the area.

The handle of the Tomahawk is a hand-picked log from the area. It is 17.4 metres long, 110 centimetres in diameter and weighs 5.4 metric tonnes. The head of the Tomahawk is made out of reinforced fibreglass. It is 5.4 metres long, 2.7 metres in diameter and weighs 1 125 kilograms. The teepee is made from concrete and forms part of the base. It is 9 metres high with a diameter of 5.4 metres.

Activity

World's Largest Tomahawk
A Saskatchewan Landmark

World's Largest Tomahawk

The **tomahawk** was a weapon used by Native people during battles many years ago.

Complete the story about the World's Largest Tomahawk with words from the box.

Print the words on the lines provided.

Cut Knife is a _____ town found in _____. A famous _____ took place here between some _____ and _____ natives many years ago.

In a _____, on the west side of Cut Knife, is the World's _____ Tomahawk. The Tomahawk is a _____ of unity and friendship between the _____ Nations and the _____ people in the area.

The _____ of the Tomahawk is a large _____. The _____ of the Tomahawk is made out of _____. The _____ is made from _____ and forms part of the base.

largest	Saskatchewan	battle	First
Cree	soldiers	park	handle
small	symbol	white	teepee
log	fibreglass	head	concrete

Information

Giant Easter Egg

An Alberta Landmark

In Vegreville, Alberta, in Elks Kinsmen Community Park, beside the fish pond, stands a huge **Pysanka** or Easter Egg. The Egg measures 7.7 metres long, 5.4 metres wide and 9.3 metres high. The Pysanka weighs 900 kilograms and rests on a 12 150 kilogram base of concrete and steel. The Egg turns in the wind like a weather vane.

The Vegreville Pysanka was designed by Professor Ronald Resch, a computer scientist at the University of Utah. He had to develop new computer programs in order to create the entire Pysanka concept. The Pysanka is like a huge jigsaw puzzle containing 524 star patterns, 2 208 equilateral triangles, 3 512 visible facets, 6 978 nuts and bolts and 177 internal struts. The Egg is recognized around the world as a unique artistic masterpiece and an achievement of nine mathematical, architectual and engineering firsts. It is the first computer modelled egg.

The Giant Easter Egg

The three colours used on the Easter Egg design are bronze, silver and gold. Bronze is the predominant colour and represents the "good earth", the land on which early settlers struggled for survival and existence. Bronze, silver and gold symbolize prosperity.

There are five distinct symbols on the design. The gold stars on each section symbolize life and good fortune. The three-pointed stars, in alternating gold and silver, symbolize the Trinity, representing the strong religious faith of Ukrainian settlers. The band of silver that travels around the Pysanka, with no beginning or end, symbolizes eternity. On the centre section of the Egg are gold and silver windmills with six vanes and points which symbolize a rich harvest. The most important symbol of the design are the silver wolf's teeth which point to the centre from the silver band. They represent the main message of protection and security given to the early settlers by the Royal Canadian Mounted Police.

A dedication message is written on a plaque in four languages: English, Ukrainian, French and German. It says "This Pysanka (Easter Egg) symbolizes the harmony, vitality and culture of the community and is dedicated as a tribute to the 100th anniversary of the Royal Canadian Mounted Police who brought peace and security to the largest multicultural settlement in all of Canada".

The Pysanka was the main attraction during the Royal Canadian Mounted Police's centennial celebrations. Thousands of tourists from around the world visit Vegreville annually and marvel at the Pysanka.

Activity Name: _____

Giant Easter Egg

An Alberta Landmark

The Giant Easter Egg

The Vegreville **Giant Easter Egg** was built to stand for the peace and security the R.C.M.P had given to the early settlers living in the town many years ago.

Complete the story about this huge Pysanka.

Print the missing words found in the box on the lines provided.

The Giant Easter _____ is found in a _____ in Vegreville, Alberta. It is a _____ Easter Egg called a _____. The Egg was designed on a _____. It looks like a huge _____ puzzle. There are 524 _____ patterns, 2 208 equilateral _____ and 3 512 other _____ on the Egg.

There are three _____ on the Egg. They are _____, _____ and _____. Bronze is the _____ colour and stands for the _____. All three colours stand for _____.

_____ kinds of _____ are seen on the Egg. The gold stars on each _____ stand for _____ and good _____. The three-_____ stars stand for the _____ the settlers had in God. The silver _____ stands for eternity. The silver _____ represent a good _____. The silver _____ teeth stand for the way the R.C.M.P. _____ the early settlers.

The Pysanka was built to _____ the one hundred year _____ of the R.C.M.P.

park	Ukrainian	wealth	bronze	main
star	Pysanka	computer	symbols	silver
shapes	colours	triangles	pointed	Five
Egg	earth	jig-saw	band	gold
life	faith	fortune	harvest	end
wolf's	celebrate	windmills	protected	birthday

Information

Badlands and Bones

An Alberta Landmark

Alberta's Badlands

In an area along the Red Deer River, between the towns of Brooks and Drumheller, eroded cliffs, hoodoos and a miniature canyon have been carved out of the prairie itself by retreating glaciers. Large and intricate drainage channels have been carved through the soft rock by immense amounts of water as well.

The **Badlands** are similar to a desert and in the spring they come to life as the prickly pear and pincushion cactus explode into fiery red and yellow flowers. Along the river valley many species of birds and wildlife make their homes.

As you wander away from the river's edge, the ground becomes dry and cracked. The landscape is stark and looks moonlike. One area in the Badlands called **Dinosaur Provincial Park** is known as the "Valley of the Moon".

The Badlands are a great place to explore, but only in good weather. Many areas are underlain by a bentonite clay soil. The clay swells and forms a completely frictionless surface when wet. The clay also causes flash floods through the normally dry valley.

Dinosaur Provincial Park is found in the Badlands. At one time, this area was a lush flood plain not far from the great Bearspaw Sea. Over millions of years, the river left behind layers of sediment much like the pages of a book, each layer telling the story of a different period in the history of this amazing site. Today, these clay, mud and sand deposits are known as the Judith River Formation and are famous all over the world for their bone deposits.

Many dinosaurs roamed this flood plain looking for food. Large plant-eaters such as the duck-billed "Parasaurolophus" used their flat bills to eat the leaves on the tall trees that grew along the flood plain. Quite often, these docile plant-eaters fell prey to the vicious "Albertosaurus" or its equally hungry relatives. Sometimes, the remains of their prey were buried beneath the sediments only to reappear millions of years later to the delight of paleontologists. Many of the prey have teeth from their hunter embedded in their bones.

Exploring Dinosaur National Park can be very exciting as there are endless varieties of bone and fossil fragments as nature continually uncovers the remains of animals lost millions of years ago. The bones may be looked at but must be left where they are found.

Activity

Badlands and Bones
An Alberta Landmark

Alberta's Badlands

The **Alberta Badlands** are located in dinosaur territory along the Red Deer River.

How well did you listen?

Read each sentence carefully.

Print **True** or **False** on the line provided at the end of each sentence.

1. The Badlands are covered with green grass, tall trees and beautiful flowers. _____

2. The Badlands are found between the towns of Calgary and Lethbridge. _____

3. The Badlands are dry and look very much like a desert. _____

4. The land in the Badlands looks like the surface of the moon. _____

5. It is safe to explore the Badlands in all kinds of weather. _____

6. At one time, dinosuars lived in the Badlands. _____

7. In Dinosaur Provincial Park, people can hunt for dinosaur bones for souvenirs to take home. _____

8. Animals and birds are not able to live in the Badlands. _____

9. Hoodoos, cliffs and a canyon are found in the Alberta Badlands. _____

10. The Peace River flows through the Badlands. _____

Information

Head-Smashed-In Buffalo Jump

An Alberta Landmark

Head-Smashed-In Buffalo Jump

Head-Smashed-In Buffalo Jump was chosen to be a World Heritage Site in 1981. It is one of the oldest, largest and best-preserved buffalo jump sites in North America. A buffalo jump is a high area or cliff over which buffalo were stampeded by Native hunters.

Long before the white man came to settle in North America, the prairies were home to large herds of wandering buffalo. They grazed on the plentiful grasses of the plains and they were the life blood of many of the earliest residents. Ancestors of the Blackfoot nation hunted the buffalo long before the white man introduced horses and guns. In those days, dogs were used as pack animals. Small bands of Native people would move camp as many as 50 times a year to follow the wandering herds.

The buffalo meant everything to the Native people and the best hunting sites were kept a secret. The early people had to develop creative ways of hunting such dangerous animals. Long lines of "stone cairns" (markers) were built to help the hunters direct the buffalo to the "cliff kill site". Thousands of these small stones piles were placed along the drive lanes that led to a gathering basin. The hunters would hide behind the markers.

To begin the hunt, "Buffalo Runners", young Native hunters, would imitate the bleating sound of a lost calf in order to get the herd moving. As the buffalo moved closer to the "drive lanes" the hunters would circle behind and upwind of the herd and scare the animals by shouting and waving robes. The frightened buffalo stampeded towards the edge of the cliff. The animals at the front of the herd would try to stop at the edge but the sheer weight of the herd pressing from behind would force the buffalo over the cliff. As many as three hundred buffalo could die in a few minutes. The bottom of the cliff is called the "kill site".

The flat area below the kill site was where the hunters camped while they finished butchering the buffalo. The meat was sliced into thin strips and hung on racks to dry in the sun. Meat was also used to make "pemmican". Grease, bone marrow and sometimes berries were pounded together with the dried meat to preserve it.

The name "Head-Smashed-In" had nothing to do with buffalo. It describes the story of a curious young brave. The Native name for this place is "Estipah sikini kots" which means "where he got his head smashed in".

According to a Piegan Native tale, about 150 years ago, a young brave wanted to get a closer look at the slaughter of the buffalo. The brave climbed into a hollow in the cliff. Here he had a perfect view of the buffalo cascading past him to their death. Unfortunately for him, the hunt was unusually good that day and when he was freed from the cliff, his head and been crushed between the rock face and the carcasses of the buffalo.

Today at the Interpretive Centre, tourists can stand on top of the cliffs that provided the last living view for untold number of buffalo. Perhaps they can hear the sound of thundering hooves made by immense herds of buffalo in the distance.

Activity   Name: _____

Head-Smashed-In Buffalo Jump
An Alberta Landmark

Imagine watching a herd of thundering buffalo falling over a cliff to their deaths. This kind of event took place many years ago at a place called **Head-Smashed-In Buffalo Jump**.

Use the word **before** or the word **after** to complete each sentence below.

Head-Smashed-In buffalo Jump

1. The buffalo herds were grazing on prairie grasses _____ the white man came to settle North America.
2. The Native people hunted the buffalo _____ the white man brought horses and guns.
3. Native hunters would circle behind and upwind of the herd _____ the buffalo began to move.
4. The Buffalo Runners would make the sound of a lost calf _____ the herd began to move.
5. The buffalo would begin running _____ the hunters shouted and waved robes at them.
6. The buffalo at the front of the herd tried to stop _____ they fell over the cliff.
7. The buffalo died _____ they fell over the cliff.
8. A young brave climbed into a hollow in a cliff _____ the buffalo hunt.
9. The young brave was found dead _____ the buffalo hunt.
10. The thundering hooves of many buffalo could be heard _____ they fell over the cliff.

On another sheet of paper, draw a picture to show part of the buffalo hunt.

© S&S Learning Materials   SSJ1-51

Information

Barkerville Historic Town

A British Columbia Landmark

Billy Barker, Prospector

Barkerville Historic Town is located in the Cariboo Mountains, 80 kilometres east of Quesnel in British Columbia. In 1862, Billy Barker found gold at Williams Creek and this discovery began the famous Cariboo Gold Rush. Thousands of people travelled the Cariboo Wagon Trail between 1862 and 1870 converging on the boomtown. During the gold rush days, Barkerville was the largest town in the Canadian West.

Barkerville grew beside the Barker claims. Crude cabins and tents of the miners made way for more permanent log and frame buildings. Businesses such as saloons, dancehalls, general stores and boarding houses served the needs of the miners. The buildings were built upon posts to avoid the mud, and wooden plank sidewalks were built for people to walk on.

Food and supplies were carried to the Cariboo on miner's backs or by pack trains. In time, the Cariboo Wagon Road was built to transport goods by wagons and people in stagecoaches.

The social life in Barkerville was noisy and exciting. "Hurdy Gurdy" girls danced with the miners for a dollar a dance in the dance halls. Gambling and drinking were activities enjoyed by the miners in the saloons. Horse races and prize fights were common activities as well. Barkerville continued to be a thriving little town until the turn of the century.

Today, Barkerville lives on as a town of discovery with 120 reconstructed buildings on display. Interpreters and a troupe of actors portray characters from Barkerville's past to give visitors a first hand experience of life in the Gold Rush era. Wild stories and lively songs enjoyed by miners over 100 years ago can still be heard at the Theatre Royal. Famous Judge Begbee, a professional actor, retells the story of the struggle to bring British justice to the wild frontier in British Columbia in the Richfield Courthouse.

On the banks of Williams Creek, the massive "Cornish Wheel" is put into operation. Daniel Grimsby and Jack Beaman, early miners, demonstrate how the wheel works. Everyone loves to watch the town blacksmith at work making his anvil sing with the blows of his mighty hammer as he turns some iron into a tool or implement. The delicious smell of sourdough bread often entices visitors into the local bake shop for a taste. Foamy old-style root beer may be sipped in the saloon of the hotel. Travelling through town in a stagecoach shows the sights and sounds that early Gold Rush travellers experienced on their arrival.

Activity

Barkerville Historic Town

A British Columbia Landmark

Billy Barker, Prospector

Follow the Gold Rush Trail that leads to **Barkerville**, the town that gold built.

Read each sentence about Barkerville carefully.

Decide if the sentence tells Who?, What?, Why?, When?, Where? or How? during the Gold Rush.

Print the correct word on the line at the end of each sentence.

Who?	What?	Where?	Why?	When?	How?

1. During the Gold Rush days, Barkerville was a large town. _____
2. Barkerville is located in the Cariboo Mountains in British Columbia. _____
3. Billy Barker found gold at Williams Creek. _____
4. The buildings in Barkerville were built on posts to keep away from the mud. _____
5. Food and supplies were carried on the backs of miners or by pack trains. _____
6. The buildings in Barkerville were used for saloons, dancehalls, stores and homes. _____
7. Barkerville grew beside the gold claim of Billy Barker. _____
8. The Cariboo Road was built for wagons and stagecoaches to travel on. _____
9. Hurdy Gurdy girls charged the miners a dollar a dance. _____
10. Barkerville Historic Town has 120 buildings to visit. _____
11. Barkerville is open all year for tourists to visit. _____
12. Actors dress up as people from the past and sing songs and tell stories to the tourists. _____

Information

Queen Charlotte Islands

A British Columbia Landmark

The **Queen Charlotte Islands** are located in the Pacific Ocean off the coast of British Columbia. There are 1 884 islands in the archipelago (a group of islands). Seven of the largest islands are - from north to south-Langara, Graham, Moresby, Louise, Lyell, Burnaby and Kunghit Island. The two main islands are Graham Island and Moresby Island which are separated by the very narrow Skidgate Channel. The population of the Islands is approximately 6 000 inhabitants.

The Islands in the archipelago are covered with a mixture of snow-topped mountains, misty forests and windswept sandy beaches. Their coastlines are cut with deep fiords that plunge into the sea. The total land area of the Queen Charlotte Islands is approximately 9 984 square kilometres and stretches 250 kilometres from north to south.

The Queen Charlotte Islands are also called "Haida Gwaii", islands of the people, and have been home to the Haida people for at least 7 000 years. At one time, approximately 14 000 people lived in 126 known village sites. Europeans discovered the islands and brought the disease smallpox to the Haida people. Many of the people died from the disease. The Haida left their villages and moved to Skidgate. Many of these abandoned villages contain the best remaining examples of original native totem poles in the world. The Haida village called "Ninstints" has been declared as a World Heritage Site in recognition of the history of mankind.

The Queen Charlotte Islands are often called the "Canadian Galopagos" due to their evolutionary showcase. Theories suggest that parts of the Islands escaped the last ice age, forming a glacial refuge for certain forms of plant and animal life. There are plant species and different sub-species of birds, fish and mammals found nowhere else in the world.

Millions of seabirds use the Islands as breeding colonies due to immense amounts of plankton during the spring and early summer. Some of the colourful species seen are tufted puffins, horned puffins, rhinoceros auklets, black-footed albatross, black oyster catchers and pigeon guillemots. Along the coast, bald eagles and their nests can be seen. The saw-whet owl is one of the unique island sub-species.

Blue, sperm, minke, sei, gray, finback, humpback and killer whales all frequent the waters around the Queen Charlotte Islands. They feed on the large areas of plankton in the waters.

Steller sea lions congregate at the southern tip of the Queen Charlotte Islands to mate and give birth to their pups. This is one of the largest breeding rookeries on the west coast of North America. Harbour Seals are frequently seen either swimming near shore or lying on beaches.

The Queen Charlotte Islands' black bear is the largest black bear in the world. Black-tailed deer and raccoons were species introduced to the Islands. Unfortunately, they are causing many ecological problems. They do not have natural predators and are increasing in numbers. The raccoons steal eggs and young from bird colonies and the deer are over-browsing the cedar trees.

The forests on the Islands are filled with giant stands of sitka spruce, western hemlock, red and yellow cedar. The floors of the forests are deeply carpeted with a hundred types of mosses, salal bushes, huckleberry and ferns.

This quiet wilderness of beautiful islands offers an escape to a roughly-edged paradise. There are countless beaches, streams, fishing holes, coves and abandoned Haida villages to explore. Visitors who come to visit these enchanting islands will never forget their visit.

Activity

Name: _____

Queen Charlotte Islands
A British Columbia Landmark

There are many things to see when you visit the **Queen Charlotte** Islands.

In the word search, **circle** the names of the sights you would see on the Islands.

In the totem pole, print the name of each one found. There are **20** sights to find.

```
K A J B I C H D B G E F F C G B H A I Z J Y K
N T O T E M P O L E S M E L D P U F F I N S X
O N P O Q O P R A Q S R T S U T V U W V X W Y
M Z L A K U B J C C I D H F E R N S G E F F E
P U O V N N W M K X L Y K O Z J A I B H C G D
T Q S R R T S Q B P T O U R N V M W L X K Y J
A E B D C A D C E F B G A E H Z M O S S E S I
Z F Y G X I W H A V I U J S T K S L R M Q E N
X G W H V N I U R J T K S T L R M Q N P O A P
F Y E Z D S C I S L A N D S B A A B Z C Y L X
H N I M J L K K L J M I N H O G P F Q E R S D
U W H A L E S S O T B A L D E A G L E S V P W
L J K K J L I M H N G O F P E Q D R C S B T A
I B E A C H E S M H N G R A C C O O N S O F P
B U A V Z W Y X X Y W Z V U A T B S C R D Q E
M H A I D A V I L L A G E S L O K S N J M I L
N P O Q P R Q S R T S U T E V U W P V X W Y X
Y H Z G A F B E C D D C E A F B G R H A D I Z
O C E D A R T R E E S I N L M J L U K K E L J
P V Q U R T S S T R U Q V I P W O C X N E Y M
G A L B A T R O S S F W E O D X C E B Y R A F
H H I G J F K E L D M C N N O B P T Q A R Z I
I C J B K A L Z M Y N X O S W P V R Q U R T O
D D E C F B G A H Z I Y J X K W L E V M U N R
T S A W W H E T O W L S E S F R G E Q H P I D
U J V K W L X M Y N Z O A P B Q C S R D S E S
```

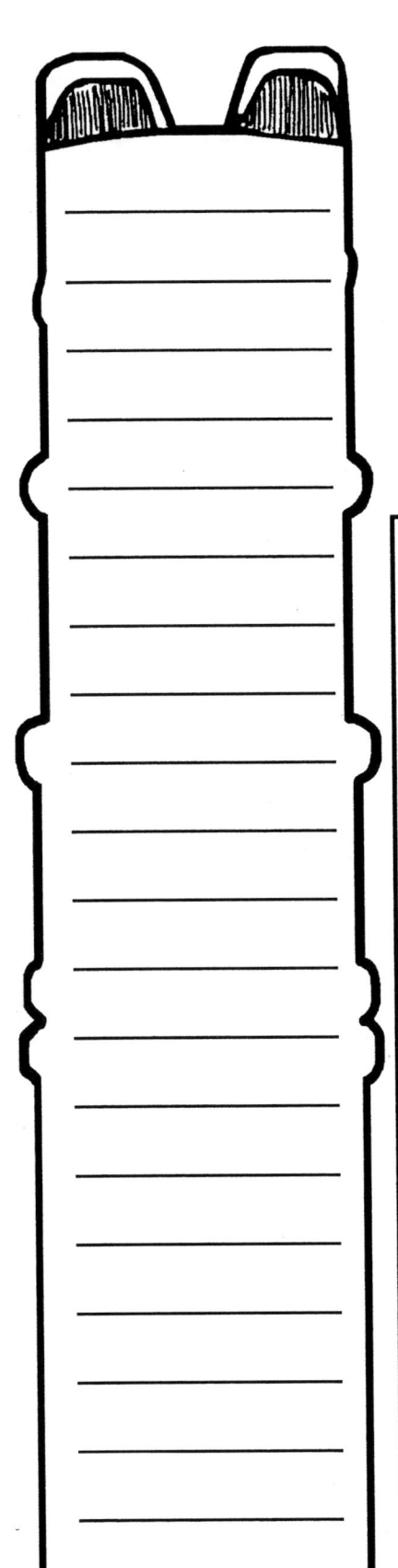

© S&S Learning Materials 61 SSJ1-51

Information

Vancouver's Bridges

British Columbia's Landmarks

The **Lion's Gate Bridge** spans the First Narrows of Burrard Inlet in the city of Vancouver, British Columbia. The bridge was named after the twin snow-capped peaks that stand like guardians over the harbour below. The peaks are known as the "Lions" and were the inspiration for the name of the new bridge. A sculptor was hired to create a monument to both the bridge and the peaks. On either side of the Lion's Gate Bridge's south entrance stand large stone lions. On May 19, 1939, King George VI and Queen Elizabeth, his wife, attended the official opening.

The Lion's Gate Bridge

The Lion's Gate Bridge is one of the oldest and best used of the fifteen bridges in Vancouver. The three-lane bridge carries 25 million vehicle trips per year. The Lion's Gate Bridge spans the entrance to Vancouver Harbour, Canada's gateway to the Pacific Rim.

The **Capilano Suspension Bridge** is also located in Vancouver, British Columbia. The 35 metre suspension bridge is stretched across a canyon 69 metres above Vancouver's spectacular Capilano River. Although it often sways and creaks in the wind, it is able to support the weight of ten heavy duty military fighter planes. More than 850 000 visitors cross it each year.

The Capilano Suspension Bridge

The original Capilano Suspension Bridge was built by George MacKay in the late 1800s. With the help of local natives and a team of horses, he suspended a hemp rope and cedar plank bridge across the river. Natives called it the "laughing bridge" because of the noise it made when the wind blew through the canyon. George MacKay had a dream to develop the area as a recreational wonderland but died before he could see it actually take place.

In 1903, the hemp rope bridge was replaced by a wire cable bridge. In 1910, Edward Mahon bought the property and developed the town of North Vancouver and established the Capilano Suspension Bridge as a major recreational attraction. Since then, various owners have improved the site making it a popular tourist attraction.

Today, visitors can view the colourful totem poles that are on display and watch First Nation Carvers work while they tell their ancient stories. They can take a walk on the suspension bridge to the other side of the canyon to view the plants and animals found in the West Coast Rainforest.

Activity

Name: _____

Vancouver's Bridges

British Columbia's Landmarks

1. *The Lion's Gate Bridge*

2. *The Capilano Suspension Bridge*

If the sentence describes the Lion's Gate Bridge, **print** the **numeral 1** in the box.

If the sentence describes the Capilano Suspension Bridge, **print** the **numeral 2** in the box.

☐ This bridge was named after two snow-capped mountains.

☐ This bridge is 35 metres long.

☐ The first bridge was made from rope and cedar planks.

☐ Two stone lions sit on either side of the south entrance to this bridge.

☐ The rope bridge was stretched across a canyon and a river.

☐ It took people and a team of horses to build this bridge.

☐ This bridge is used by cars, trucks and other vehicles to cross a harbour.

☐ The Native people living in the area called this bridge the "laughing bridge".

☐ Every year, thousands of tourists visit this bridge and watch First Nations carvers at work.

☐ It is the oldest and best used bridge in Vancouver.

Information

Stern-wheelers of the Far North

Yukon Territory Landmarks

At one time there were about 350 stern-wheelers on the Yukon River and other major rivers in the Yukon Territory. They were described as a paddle-wheel steamer with a stern wheel instead of a side wheel. These large wooden boats travelled the northern rivers for almost 100 years carrying supplies, equipment, ore and passengers. They chugged up and down the Yukon River, from after breakup until just before the river froze in the winter.

The Yukon stern-wheelers were similar to the river boats that travelled on the Missouri River. They had flat hulls for speed and "hog posts" on the upper decks to prevent twisting and to haul the boats over shallow spots along the river. The boats were made out of Douglas fir, cedar and pine which was economical to use as many ships were lost to snags, rocks, sandbars, ice floes, rapids and other river hazards.

A typical stern-wheeler was about 51 metres long, 10.5 metres wide and could carry up to 225 tonnes of cargo. They were run by locomotive-type boiler engines and burned large amounts of wood. On a trip from Whitehorse to Dawson, a stern-wheeler would burn 120 cords of wood. Wood camps were established along the river to provide fuel for the boats.

In time, airplanes and all-weather roads ended the stern-wheelers role in the Yukon. Bridges built along the highway were too low and the old river steamers could not pass under them and all were beached.

There were only two grand old riverboats that survived in the Yukon. They were the S.S. Klondike in Whitehorse and the S.S. Keno in Dawson City.

The S.S. Keno was the last steamer to run the Yukon River. She was 40 metres long and ten metres wide. The S.S. Keno was built in Whitehorse. She would make the run from Stewart City to Mayo Landing carrying silver, lead and zinc from the mines in the Mayo district. The ore was stock-piled on the bank of the river at Mayo Landing all winter, awaiting the arrival of the S.S. Keno in early May. In 1938, the Keno carried over 8 165 tonnes of ore. In 1960, the S.S. Keno sailed from Whitehorse to her final resting place on the riverbank in Dawson City.

The S.S. Klondike I and II were built in Whitehorse. The S.S. Klondike I was built in 1929 and could carry over 50 percent more than other boats on the river. The career of the S.S. Klondike I ended very quickly in 1936 when it ran aground in the Yukon River between Lake Laberge and the Teslin River.

The S.S. Klondike II was built immediately and looked identical to S.S. Klondike I. From 1937 to 1952, the Klondike II was used as a cargo vessel. It was the largest and last of the stern-wheelers. She carried goods and passengers on the downstream run from Whitehorse to Dawson - a distance of 740.27 kilometres in approximately 36 hours with one or two stops to take on wood. On her return run, the Klondike proceeded to Stewart Landing some 112.65 kilometres above Dawson City where sacks of silver lead ore were loaded. The upstream journey back to Whitehorse could take four or five days and six wood-stops.

The S.S. Klondike's career from cargo vessel to cruise ship took place in 1950. She was totally refurbished but the plan was twenty years too early. In August 1955, the S.S. Klondike II steamed into Whitehorse on her last run up river. Today the S.S. Klondike II has been carefully restored and now sits in permanent retirement on the bank of the Yukon River near the Robert Campbell Bridge in Whitehorse. It is the only stern-wheeler in the Yukon that is open to the public. There are over 7 000 artifacts on display.

Two grand old riverboats have survived the hazards of the Yukon rivers and the ravages of time and both are now Parks Canada National Historic Sites.

© S&S Learning Materials

Activity

Stern-wheelers of the Far North

Yukon Territory Landmarks

S.S. Klondike II

S.S. Keno

The **S.S. Keno** and the **S.S. Klondike II** are kept as memorials to all the river boats who brought goods and people to the Yukon during the Gold Rush days.

Some of the sentences below are **true** and some are **false**.

Read each sentence carefully.

On the line provided **print** either the word **true** or the word **false**.

1. A stern-wheeler is a large sailing ship used to travel on the northern rivers many years ago. _____
2. The stern-wheelers carried people, goods, machines and ore. _____
3. The stern-wheelers were made from wood and had flat bottoms with a paddle wheel at the back. _____
4. A stern-wheeler used oil to run its boiler engine. _____
5. Rocks, sandbars, rapids and ice floes often caused stern-wheelers to sink or to get stuck in the rivers. _____
6. The S.S. Klondike II ran aground in the Yukon River which ended its career as a steamer. _____
7. The S.S. Keno was the largest stern-wheeler to travel on the Yukon River. _____
8. The stern-wheelers had to stop many times on their trips to take on wood for their engines. _____
9. The S.S. Klondike II became a cruise ship and carried tourists. _____
10. The S.S. Keno rests now on a riverbank in Whitehorse. _____
11. The S.S. Klondike I and II where built exactly the same way and looked the same. _____
12. The S.S. Keno is the only stern-wheeler that is on display for tourists to visit. _____

Information

Nahanni National Park

A Northwest Territories' Landmark

Nahanni National Park

The **Nahanni-Ram Region** is located in the vast and remote southwest corner of the Northwest Territories and it is famous for its unsurpassed, spectacular wilderness. It includes the communities of Fort Simpson, Fort Liard, Wrigley, Nahanni, Butte, Jean Marie River, Trout Lake and a UNESCO World Heritage Site, **Nahanni National Park Reserve**.

This region contains some of the most rugged terrain in the in Vancouver world. No part of it is easy to reach, even today. The best way is by a charter float plane or helicopter. The two most visited spots are "Virginia Falls" and "Rabbitkettle Tufa Mounds".

Hikers, canoeists, river rafters and mountain climberscamp inside the park so they can canoe or raft the South Nahanni River, climb the Cirque of the Unclimables or the Ram Plateau. This area contains the greatest concentration of unnamed peaks and possibly the greatest unexplored wilderness in North America.

The "Ram Plateau" has rare geological formations such as "karst" topography comprised of porous limestone marked by lakes, sinkholes and thousands of unexplored caves. Some of the caves contain ice formations and animal skeletons.

Lush green mountain meadows found in this area are called "Poljes". These meadows become high, flooded lakes when water flows in faster than it can drain out. Natural hot springs bubble over tufa mounds of soft gold and cream coloured rock created by the minerals from the thermal spring water. At Rabbitkettle Hotsprings, one of the tufa mounds is 14.1 metres high and 75 metres wide. This mound is the largest one in the world. In the warm undergrowth around the sub-Arctic hot springs, wild mint and orchids grow among the spruce, balsam and popular trees.

The wildlife in the area include moose, woodland caribou, Dall sheep, rare wood bison, wolves, black bears, lynx and the fierce grizzly bear. Birds such as white pelicans, peregrine falcons, bald eagles, loons and the endangered trumpeter swan and 120 more types of birds share this area. On top of many of the tall plateaus are fossils and coral.

In the middle of the park is Virginia Falls which plunges 95 metres, or more than twice the height of Niagara Falls. It is North America's largest remaining wilderness falls.

It is not surprising that the Nahanni National Park has remained a secret and it has not been developed. Its steep terrain and unpredictable rivers and weather have made travel dangerous. During the winter, temperatures drop to -50° C. The Northern Lights help to light the dark skies as there is only three hours of sunlight each day. During the months of July and August the temperature may be as high as 23°C and the sun shines twenty hours a day.

The park was named after the mysterious "Nah'aa Native People" --- meaning "people over there far away". Prospectors did come to the area but no gold was to be found. Perhaps this is why it has not been developed.

Many legends have been told by Native People about this area. Myths about wild mountain men, a white queen, evil spirits, lost maps, lost gold and headless men are still told today. Many beautiful and dangerous natural sites bear gruesome names such as the "Funeral Range", "Death Canyon", "Headless Valley", "Hell's Gate" and Broken Skull River.

Activity Name: _____

Nahanni National Park

A Northwest Territories' Landmark

Nahanni National Park

The **Nahanni National Park** is a beautiful wilderness seen by only a few people.

Many animals, birds and land forms are found in the park.

In the box below, **underline** the words that are things you would find in Nahanni National Park.

caribou	mountains	buildings	caves
lions	waterfalls	hot springs	robins
bald eagles	roads	lakes	tulips
deserts	sinkholes	highways	caribou
valleys	maple trees	black bears	oceans
cities	meadows	gardens	moose
loons	Nahinni River	spruce trees	streets
polar bears	wood bison	horses	fossils
houses	Northern Lights	grizzly bears	wolves
plateaus	trumpeter swan	lynx	chickens

Draw pictures of **three** things that you underlined in the circles below.

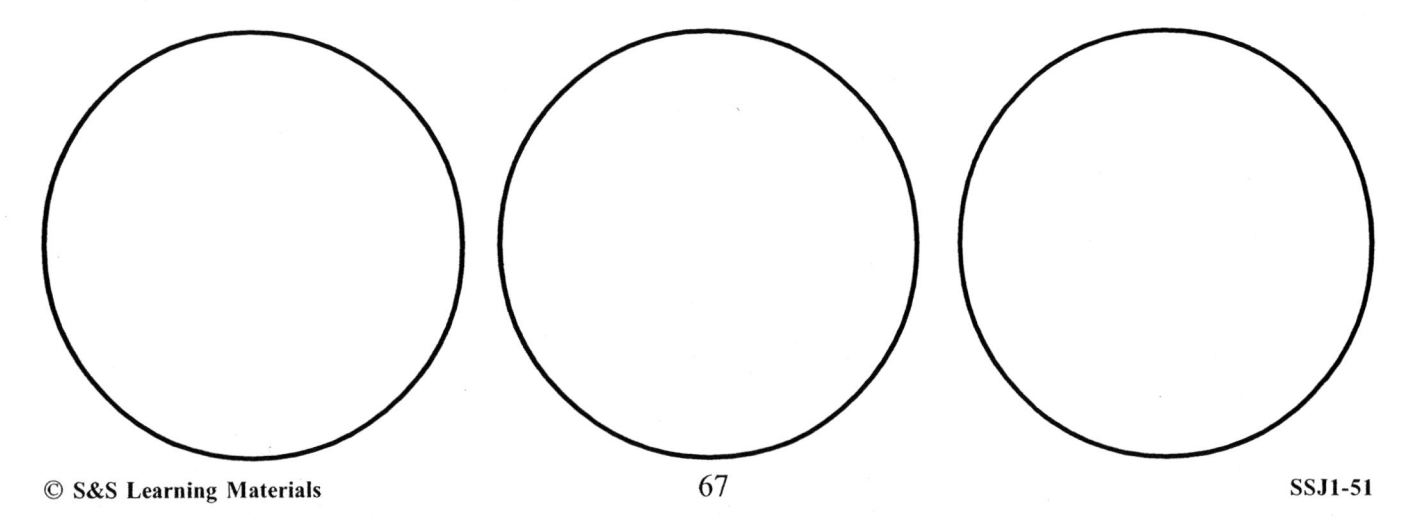

© S&S Learning Materials   67   SSJ1-51

Information

Yellowknife

A Northwest Territories Landmark

Yellowknife's Skyline

Yellowknife is the capital city of the Northwest Territories. It is located on the north shore of the Great Slave Lake and is the gateway to the Northern Frontier. It is the centre for administration, transportation and communication for the entire territory.

Yellowknife is the largest and only city in the Northwest Territories. It has a population of 17 000. The city is a mining, supply and transportation centre with an airport, radio and meteorological stations, a post of the Royal Canadian Mounted Police and federal agencies.

The town was founded in 1935 after the discovery of rich gold deposits. In 1944, another mine was discovered and a new townsite was established the next year. Yellowknife is named after a Native American tribe called the "Yellowknives" who were known for using tools made of copper.

Yellowknife is a town built on a rich gold mining heritage. In 1930, gold was discovered. The city of Yellowknife is built on top of mine tunnels that burrow deep beneath the city streets. The discovery of diamonds in 1991 at nearby Lac de Gros and the recent completion of Canada's first diamond mine, promise to continue Yellowknife's mining tradition well into the next century.

The buildings in Yellowknife are a mixture of old and new, modern and traditional. There are elegant skyscrapers and innovative houses which are built beside prospectors' shacks and quonset huts (miners' shacks).

In Yellowknife, there are wonderful walking trails that wind around a lake and wander through subarctic trees and some of the oldest rocks in the world. Outside Yellowknife, there are exciting things to do such as driving the Ingraham Trail, sailing on the Great Slave Lake or cruising on the Mackenzie River.

Yellowknife is one of the best locations in the world for viewing the "aurora borealis" or the northern lights. Tourists travel from all over the world to view the unique and beautiful northern lights. The northern lights result from forms of electromagnetic energy that are drawn to the earth's poles charging the atmosphere and causing it to glow. Yellowknife ranks number one among all Canadian cities for summer sunshine. In June alone, there are over 375 hours of sunshine.

Activity

Yellowknife

A Northwest Territories Landmark

Yellowknife's Skyline

Yellowknife is named after a Native tribe called the "Yellowknives" because they used tools made from copper.

Use the words from the box to complete the story about Yellowknife.

Print the words on the lines provided.

Yellowknife is the _____ city of the Northwest Territories. It is also the _____ and only city. Yellowknife is found on the _____ shore of the Great Slave Lake.

The _____ of Yellowknife grew when _____ was found in 1935. The city is built on top of mine _____ that are _____ under its streets. _____ huts (miners' huts) and _____ buildings sit side by side. People enjoy walking on the _____ that wander around a _____, through subarctic _____ and over some of the oldest _____ in the world.

The "aurora borealis", or the _____ lights, can best be seen in Yellowknife. During the month of _____ it receives 375 hours of _____ making it number one of all Canadian cities.

The discovery of _____ and its first diamond mine has made Yellowknife _____.

**modern
diamonds
sunshine
Quonset
famous
June
deep
city
northern
tunnels
rocks
gold
trees
north
lake
largest
trails
capital**

Information

Iqaluit: Capital of Nunavut

Nunavut's Landmark

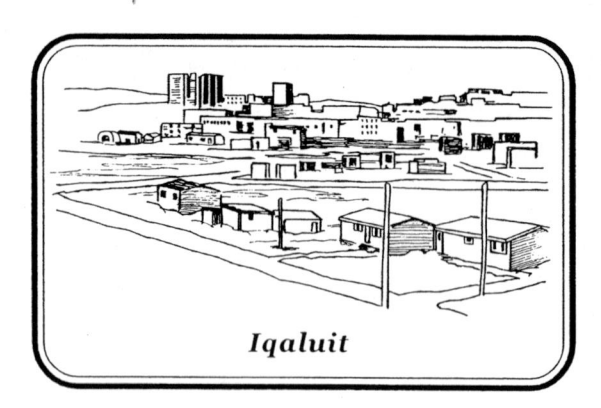

On April 1, 1999, the Territory of Nunavut was created. In December 1995, Iqaluit was selected by the residents to be the Capital of the new territory. On April 19, 2001, Iqaluit received the Order of City Status making it the most northerly capital city in Canada.

Iqaluit is located on Baffin Island, on the Frobisher Bay's coast. It is the largest and only city in Nunavut with a population of approximately 6 000 and growing steadily. The temperature in January may be -30°C and in July 15°C. In June, Iqaluit experiences a little more than five hours of darkness per day, and in December, a little more than five hours of sunlight per day. Snow does not cover the land year round and arctic weather is not always cold or miserable.

Iqaluit is a transportation hub for jet flights from Ottawa, Montreal, Yellowknife, Rankin Inlet and Greenland as well as daily services between other Nunavut communities. The airport was once a military airport and has the longest runway in the Canadian Arctic being 4 000 metres long. It not only serves airlines connecting to southern Canada but also serves as a refueling and an emergency landing site for international flights.

Buildings in Iqaluit are built on piles to prevent heat from melting the permafrost layer that lies about a metre below the surface. Iqaluit has many stores and businesses that provide the people with a wide variety of products and services. There is a hardware store, a drugstore, grocery store, banks, hospital, hotels, restaurants, churches and a museum. A theatre, swimming pool, racquet club, curling and ice arenas provide recreational activities. The Nunavut Legislative Assembly Building is located in Iqaluit. The government provides many services for the people.

There are three elementary schools and one high school in Iqaluit. There is almost no grass in the school yards but sand and gravel make a good playground. There are many sport clubs in Iqaluit such as the hockey club, the skating club, the kayak club, the skidoo club to name a few.

Although Iqaluit is a progressive city and is able to provide its residents with many of the necessities and niceties of life, the goods are very expensive. The transportation and shipping costs of the goods is very high making the prices extremely costly. For example, groceries such as eggs and milk are 50% higher in cost than the Canadian average while fast food like KFC is almost double the cost in comparison to southern Canada. Goods are usually brought by boat and unloaded during the low tide of Frobisher Bay. The hard bottom of the bay enables trucks to drive out to the boat without the fear of getting stuck.

As Iqaluit grows and industries are established in Nunavut, the lifestyle of the people and the communities will improve.

Activity Name: _____

Iqaluit: Capital of Nunavut

Nunavut's Landmark

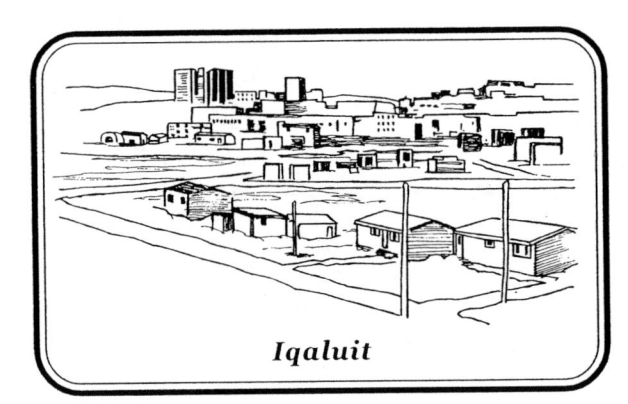

Iqaluit is the smallest capital city in Canada but is steadily growing in size.

Read each sentence below carefully.

If the sentence is a true fact, print **Yes** on the line provided.

If the sentence is a false fact, print **No** on the line provided.

Iqaluit

1. Iqaluit is found in the Yukon Territory. _____
2. It is always very cold and dark in Iqaluit. _____
3. People travel by dogsled and skidoo in the city of Iqaluit. _____
4. The houses and buildings in Iqaluit are built on piles. _____
5. You can travel by car to reach Iqaluit. _____
6. The city of Iqaluit has many kinds of stores and restaurants for the people to use. _____
7. There is no high school in Iqaluit. _____
8. Food and clothes in Iqaluit cost the same as in other parts of Canada. _____
9. The children in Iqaluit do not have sport clubs to join. _____
10. In the summer, the school playground is covered with sand and gravel. _____
11. Airplanes are in and out of Iqaluit daily. _____
12. Iqaluit is the largest and only city in the Territory of Nunavut. _____
13. In June, there are only six hours of sunlight per day. _____
14. Iqaluit has a population of only 3 000 people. _____

© S&S Learning Materials

Information

Auyuittuq National Park

A Nunavut Territory Landmark

Auyuittuq (pronounced "ow-you-ee-tuk") **National Park** is located in the Cumberland Peninsula on Baffin Island. The Park covers 19 500 square kilometres. It is filled with deep mountain valleys, dramatic fiords, ancient glaciers and spiny peaks. Auyuittuq means the "land that never melts".

Auyuittuq National Park is home to the Penny Ice Cap which is a 6 000 square kilometre ice cap left behind by the last ice age. An ice cap is a cover of ice that centres around a specific point on the surface of a piece of land. The Penny Ice Cap is huge with ice that measures 300 metres thick in places. Several major scientific studies have taken place on the Penny Ice Cap to study climatic change and global warming. Many large pieces of ice fall off the glacier each year into water and become icebergs. An iceberg is made of solid fresh water which has a lower density than salt water hence they float in the ocean. The icebergs are moulded into shapes by the wind, waves and the process of melting. About 10 000 to 30 000 are produced each year. Most of an iceberg is submerged under the water and is moved about by water currents.

Mount Thor is also found in Auyuittuq National Park. It is one of the most distinctive landmarks in the Pangnirtung Pass. Its 1 219 metre sheer cliff face attracts many climbers from around the world.

Mount Asgard is also found in the Park. This mountain is surrounded by glaciers and can only be climbed for a short time in the summer. Mount Asgard was shown in the James Bond movie called "The Spy Who Loved Me".

Auyuittuq National Park is a geologist's dream. Curled pieces of glaciers hang dangerously overhead. Loud explosions can be heard as house-sized chunks of granite crash to the valley floor in the Akshayuk Pass. Glaciers have left behind many unusual landforms such as "horns" (points of rocks shaped like a horn), "cirques" (a circular space surrounded by high rocks) and "pinnacles" (high peaks). In the Park, plants grow low to the ground such as lichens, mosses, sedges, dwarf willows and small flowering plants. Birds such as snow buntings, peregrine falcons, red polls, ptarmigans, ravens, loons, gulls and Canada geese may be seen at various times of the year in the park. Land animals that visitors often see are lemmings, ermine, foxes, arctic hares and sometimes caribou.

Visitors may tour the park by skidoo, boat or by hiking with a trained guide.

Activity

Name: _____

Auyuittuq National Park

A Nunavut Territory Landmark

Auyuittuq National Park

Auyuittuq National Park in Nunavut is filled with unusual plants, animals, birds and land forms.

Look in the word search to find these unusual sights.

Circle each one that you find. **Print** its name on the lines provided. There are **18** words to be circled.

```
M B N C O D P E Q F R G S H T I U J V K W L X M Y N Z P O A
B P E N N Y I C E C A P C G N M O U N T A I N S D Q E A P F
G E A H B I C J C K D L E L M F O G P H Q I R J S K T N L U
V A W R X L E M M I N G S A Y S M O U N T T H O R Z T G A U
B K C V D W B E X F Y G Z C H A I B J C K D L E M F N N O G
P S Q H R I E S J T K U L I C E C A P S V M P W P N X I Y O
Z R A S B T R C U D V E W E F X G Y H Z I A T J I K Q R L P
M K N J O I G P H Q G R F R S E L T D U C V A W N X Y T Z R
A L B M C N S D O E P F Q S G R I H S I T J R K N U L U M V
N H O G P F Q E R D S C T B U A C V Z W Y X M Y A Z X N A W
H C A N A D A G E E S E Z G Y F H O R N S E I D C X C G A B
I I J J K K L L M O N M O N P Q E Q U R V S G T L W U P B V
E M O S S E S D C I R Q U E S C N B S A T Z A Y E C X A W D
F P G O H N I M J L K K L J M I S N H O G P N Q S F R S E S
G Q F T E U D X C Y B B A C Z G Y H X J W L S V O U P S T Q
H A R C T I C H A R E S I D J M O U N T A S G A R D K R L S
M R N S O V P W Q Z R A S E T F U I V K W M X N Y T Z U V A
```

_____

_____

_____

_____

© S&S Learning Materials 73 SSJ1-51

Information

Famous Cabins of the North

The Yukon Territory Landmarks

The Robert Service Cabin

The Jack London Cabin

In Dawson City, Yukon, sits a little log cabin on Eighth Avenue. This was once the home to the world's famous Yukoner, Robert William Service. The cabin may have been built as early as 1897 or 1898. It is a typical cabin built in those days with logs well chinked with moss to keep out the sub-arctic cold. A double door leads into the rustic cabin. White, stark moose antlers decorate the front porch. The cabin has a sitting room, a bedroom and a very small kitchen. The roof is slanting and papered white. Over the door is nailed a horseshoe and two windows allow light to enter. The cabin is furnished with a chair made out of a tree trunk, a table, a lamp and a stool. Over the door leading to Service's bedroom hang the poet's snowshoes. In his bedroom is a narrow camp bed, a window, a small mirror and an old chest. The third room is the kitchen equipped with a Yukon stove. Here Service cooked his food, washed his dishes and arranged his shelves.

Robert Service was born in England in 1874. At the age of fifteen, he emigrated to Canada where he joined his younger brother in an experiment in ranching. He did not enjoy the life of a farmer and went to California. For the next six years, he drifted up and down the Pacific Coast. In 1903, he had no money and took a job with the Canadian Bank of Commerce in Vancouver. Later, he was sent to Whitehorse in the Yukon Territory, then to Dawson City to work as a bank clerk.

While living in this log cabin, which he never owned, he was inspired to write some of his most famous poems and a book called "The Trail of 98" which became a Hollywood motion picture. Service was known as the "Bard of the Yukon" who immortalized the Klondike Gold Rush in such classics as "The Shooting of Dan McGrew" and the "Cremation of Sam McGee".

In 1912, Service accepted the job of war correspondent in the Balkan War. During his travels in Europe, Service married a woman from Paris and purchased a villa in Brittany. In the First World War, he served as an American volunteer ambulance unit and became a war correspondent for the Canadian government. After the war, he travelled and wrote many poems and several novels. During World War II, he escaped from Poland to Hollywood where he lived in exile until the end of the war and then returned to France. Although he never returned to the Yukon after he left in 1912, it always remained a part of his life until his death in 1958.

Information Card 2 *Famous Cabins of the North*

Robert Service

Jack London

Jack London was an American author who wrote 50 books and over 1 000 articles from 1899 until his death in 1916. His most famous stories were written about the Klondike in a cabin in the Yukon.

The original cabin was built on the North Fork of Henderson Creek, 120 kilometres south of Dawson City, just prior to the gold rush of 1898.

Jack London dropped out of school at the age of fourteen and worked at various jobs such as oyster pirate, seal hunter, fisheries patrolman, a dockhand and a rail-riding hobo. He travelled across Canada and the United States on the rails (by train) during the great depression. London saw the pain and suffering experienced by people during that period.

In July 1897, he and his brother-in-law went to the Yukon to look for gold. Although he never struck it rich, he turned his Klondike adventures into fame and fortune with his famous short stories which he wrote in his cabin.

After the gold rush, his cabin was abandoned. In 1936, a group of trappers travelling in the area discovered London's signature on a log on the back wall of the cabin. It said "Jack London, miner and author, Jan. 27, 1898". One of the trappers carefully removed the signature with his axe for safekeeping.

Yukon author, Dick North organized a search for the cabin in 1965 and eventually found it. He had the cabin dismantled and shipped out. From the logs of the one cabin, two identical cabins were made. One was to stay in Dawson City and is located on Eighth and Firth Street while the other one was shipped to the Jack London Square in Oakland California, London's hometown.

The cabin in Dawson City contains photos, documents, newspaper articles and other London memorabilia. Dick North spends his summers as an interpreter at the Jack London Cabin to share his knowledge with thousands of visitors from around the world.

Activity   Name: _____

Famous Cabins of the North

The Yukon Territory Landmarks

Robert Service and **Jack London** were famous authors who wrote many famous poems and stories about the Klondike during the gold rush days.

Below are some sentences about both authors.

Read each sentence carefully.

If the sentence is about Robert Service, **print** his name on the line provided.

If the sentence is about Jack London, **print** his name on the line provided.

Robert Service Cabin

Jack London Cabin

1. _____ wrote wonderful, exciting stories about life in the Yukon.
2. _____ was born in England and came to Canada when he was fifteen.
3. _____ wrote mainly poems about people and life in the Yukon.
4. The _____ cabin was found by trappers travelling in the area.
5. _____ worked as a bank teller in Dawson City.
6. _____ was a hobo who hitch-hiked rides on trains that travelled all across Canada and the United States.
7. _____ wrote his name on a log in his cabin.
8. The _____ Cabin has a sitting room, a bedroom and a very small kitchen.
9. There are two _____ cabins, one in Dawson City and one in Oakland, California.
10. _____ wrote the famous poem called "The Cremation of Sam McGee".

© S&S Learning Materials

Answer Key

Cape Spear: *(page 7)*
Paragraph One: bonfires, harbours, guide, safely, warn, dangers
Paragraph Two: towers, beacons, Candles, oil lamps, kerosene
Paragraph Three: lighthouse, Cape Spear, St. John's, 75, square, tower, electricity, flashed
Paragraph Four: soldiers, bunker, guns, tip, protect, German
Paragraph Five: whales, icebergs, seabirds, ships

L'Anse Aux Meadows: *(page 9)*
Paragraph One: viking, explored, lived, coast, Columbus, salmon, timber, grapes
Paragraph Two: trip, travelled, community, Meadows, sod, forge, iron, Greenland, rotted, overgrown
Paragraph Three: site, eight, lower, walls
Paragraph Four: re-created, houses, Historic, Heritage

Gros Morne National Park: *(page 11)*
Paragraph One: largest, western, Newfoundland, valleys, peninsulas, fiords
Paragraph Two: oldest, million, squeezed, continents, collided, trilobites
Paragraph Three: moose, foxes, bears, hares, caribou, eagles, osprey, seals, whales
Paragraph Four: Tourists, hike, photograph, observe, look, hunt, watch, icebergs

Green Gables: *(page 13)*
Paragraph One: Green, setting, Anne, Gables, white, house, restored, furnished
Paragraph Two: barn, woodshed, Haunted, Lane, Hollow
Paragraph Three: never, grew, explored
Paragraph Four: tourists, visit, walk, trails

Province House: *(page 15)*
Paragraph One: Province House, Charlottetown, Island, built, government
Paragraph Two: three-storey, stone, conference, joining, provinces, country, confederation, birthplace
Paragraph Three: Tourists, view

Acadian Historical Village: *(page 17)*
Paragraph One: French, world, Acadie
Paragraph Two: New Brunswick, Caraquet, buildings, homes
Paragraph Three: 50, timbers, one, loft, sleeping, eating, working, poor, furniture, weave, spin, prepare, greet, answer
Paragraph Four: tourists, cooper's, lobster, tinsmith's, newspaper

Kings Landing Historical Settlement: *(page 19)*

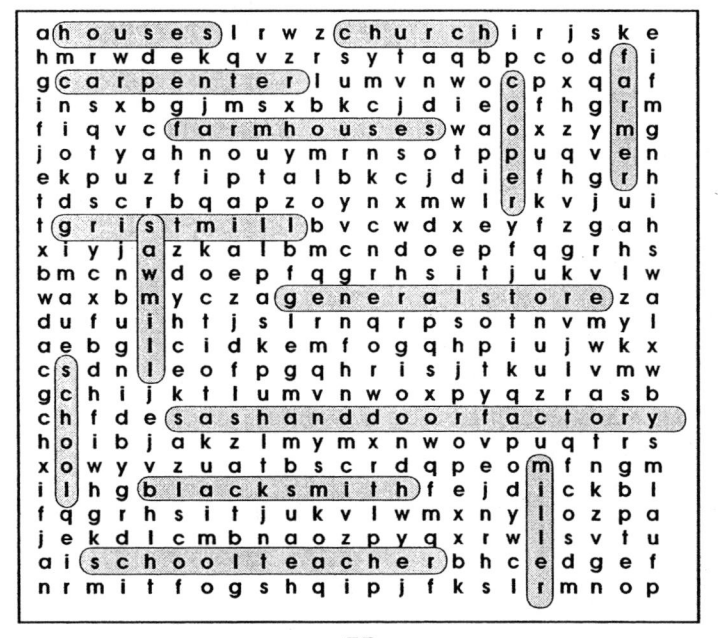

The Hartland Covered Bridge: *(page 21)*
1. In 2001, the Hartland Covered Bridge was 100 years old.
2. The Bridge spans the Saint John River.
3. The Hartland Covered Bridge is found in Hartland, New Brunswick.
4. It is the longest covered bridge in the world.
5. The citizens from the two communities gave money to build the Bridge.
6. Wooden bridges were often covered to protect them from all kinds of weather.
7. A local doctor was the first citizen to cross the Bridge.
8. In 1980, the Hartland Covered Bridge was declared a National Historic Site.
9. The Hartland Covered Bridge measures 390 metres long.
10. Later, a side walkway was added so people could walk across the Bridge.

Fundy Bay and the Hopewell Rocks: *(page 23)*
Each illustration will vary.

Alexander Graham Bell Historic Park: *(page 25)*
Paragraph One: Scotland, Brantford, famous, telephone
Paragraph Two: mountains, holidays, village, Baddeck, scenery, cool, summer, Bhreagh, mountain, large, eleven
Paragraph Three: daughters, inventions, writings

Halifax Citadel National Historic Site: *(page 27)*
1. British 2. Royal Navy 3. supplies 4. navy ships 5. French
6. star-shaped 7. bagpipe 8. barracks 9. garrison cells 10. cannon firing

Peggy's Cove: *(page 29)*
1. fishing 2. carved, granite 3. tower, wood 4. keeper 5. lamp
6. second, concrete 7. stories, name 8. colour, white, green 9. Point, warn, post office
10. lantern, red

Montmorency Falls Park: *(page 31)*
1. Samuel de Champlain 2. 83 metres 3. Niagara Falls 4. a beautiful villa
5. lonely 6. to get married 7. Queen Victoria 8. an inn
9. a cable car 10. 487 steps

Quebec City: **(page 33)**
The following sentences should have a checkmark in its box.
In Upper Town there is a fort called the Citadel.
Old Quebec City is made of Upper Town and Lower Town.
Upper Town and Lower Town have a stone wall with gates around them.
On the Plains of Abraham, a big battle took place between the French and the English.
Lower Town is the place where the early settlers lived.
The English won the battle that took place on the Plains of Abraham.
The Van Doos are a French Speaking Regiment of the Canadian Military and make the Citadel their base.

Percé Rock: *(page 35)*
Paragraph One: Rock, visit, size, beautiful, long, wide, high, weighs, million, hole, ocean, fossils, walk

Niagara Falls: *(page 37)*
Paragraph One: Niagara, Ontario, Erie
Paragraph Two: Horseshoe, American
Paragraph Three: attracts, steamers, Maid of the Mist, churning, water, electricity
Paragraph Four: museums
Paragraph Five: Marineland, whales, seals

Niagara Falls Legend: *(page 39)*
1. She had to marry an old ugly man.
2. She jumped into her canoe and floated down the river.
3. He knew that her boat would be smashed on the rocks below.
4. The snake monster poisoned the drinking water.
6. The dead monster's body blocked the narrow part of the river causing the river to rise above it and fall down.
7. Pictures will vary.

Ste. Marie Among the Hurons: *(page 41)*
Paragraph One: priests, Hurons, God, mission, Ste. Marie, bakery, chapel, hospital
Paragraph Two: wilderness, corn, fish
Paragraph Three: ten, war, attacked, tortured, killed
Paragraph Four: burn, destroy

The CN Tower: *(page 43)*
1. False   2. True   3. False   4. False   5. True   6. False   7. True
8. True   9. False   10. True   11. False   12. True   13. False   14. True

Mennonite Heritage Village: *(page 45)*
1. semlin   2. summer kitchen   3. log house   4. church   5. public school
6. blacksmith shop   7. general store   8. farm barn and pens   9. printery
10. windmill

York Factory National Historic Site: *(page 47)*
Paragraph One: River, Manitoba, trading, furs
Paragraph Two: years, oldest, frozen, permafrost
Paragraph Three: three, stone, brick, heaving, pressure

The Big Muddy Badlands: *(page 49)*
Paragraph One: Saskatchewan, border, valley, Muddy, hills, smooth, grass, buttes, cliffs, ridges
Paragraph Two: steep, alone, Castle
Paragraph Three: lived, hunted, deer, coyotes, foxes, weasels, eagles, falcons, hawks, cactus, wildflowers

World's Largest Tomahawk: *(page 51)*
Paragraph One: small, Saskatchewan, battle, soldiers, Cree
Paragraph Two: park, Largest, symbol, First, white
Paragraph Three: handle, log, head, fibreglass, teepee, concrete

Giant Easter Egg: *(page 53)*
Paragraph One: Egg, park, Ukrainian, Pysanka, computer, jigsaw, star, triangles, shapes
Paragraph Two: colours, bronze, silver, gold, main, earth, wealth
Paragraph Three: five, symbols, end, life, fortune, pointed, faith, band, windmills, harvest, wolf's, protected
Paragraph Four: celebrate, anniversary

Badlands and Bones: *(page 55)*
1. False   2. False   3. True   4. True   5. False   6. True   7. False   8. False   9. True   10. False

Head-Smashed-In Buffalo Jump: *(page 57)*
1. before   2. before   3. after   4. before   5. after
6. before   7. after   8. before   9. after   10. before

Barkerville Historic Town: *(page 59)*
1. When   2. Where   3. Who   4. Why   5. How   6. What
7. Where   8. Why   9. Who   10. What   11. When   12. Who

Queen Charlotte Islands: *(page 61)*

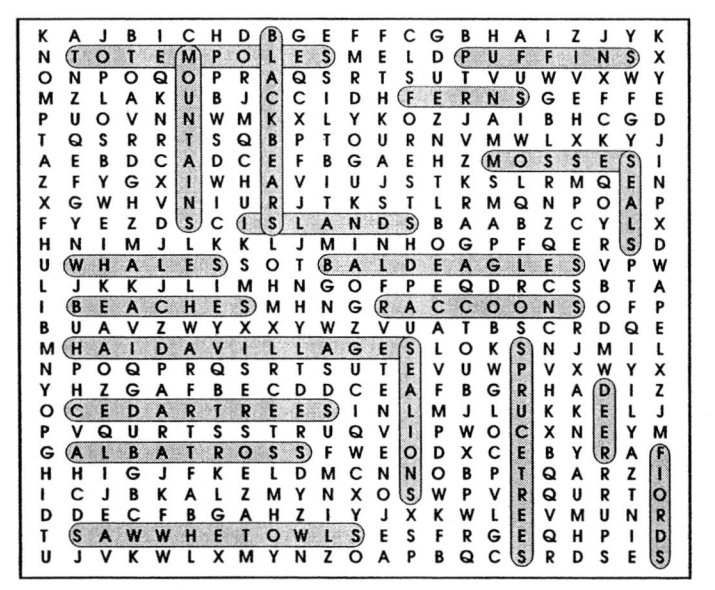

Vancouver's Bridges: *(page 63)*
Answers are in order from top to bottom - 1, 2, 2, 1, 2, 2, 1, 2, 2, 1

Stern-wheelers of the Far North: *(page 65)*
1. False   2. True   3. True   4. False   5. True   6. False
7. False   8. True   9. True   10. False   11. True   12. False

Nahanni National Park: *(page 67)*
Words to be underlined.
Column One: caribou, bald eagles, valleys, loons, plateaus
Column Two: mountains, waterfalls, sinkholes, meadows, Nahanni River, wood bison, Northern Lights, trumpeter swan
Column Three: hot springs, lakes, black bears, spruce trees, grizzly bears, lynx
Column Four: caves, caribou, moose, fossils, wolves

Yellowknife: *(page 69)*
Paragraph One: capital, largest, north
Paragraph Two: city, gold, tunnels, deep, Quonset, modern, trails, lake, trees, rocks
Paragraph Three: northern, June, sunshine
Paragraph Four: diamonds, famous

Iqaluit: Capital of Nunavut: *(page 71)*
1. No   2. No   3. No   4. Yes   5. No   6. Yes   7. No
8. No   9. No   10. Yes   11. Yes   12. Yes   13. No   14. No

Auyuittuq National Park: *(page 73)*

Famous Cabins of the North: *(page 76)*
1. Jack London   2. Robert Service   3. Robert Service   4. Jack London
5. Robert Service   6. Jack London   7. Jack London   8. Robert Service
9. Jack London   10. Robert Service

Publication Listing

See Dealer or www.sslearning.com For Pricing 1-800-463-6367

Code #	Title and Grade
SSC1-12	A Time of Plenty Gr. 2
SSN1-92	Abel's Island NS Gr. 4-6
SSF1-16	Aboriginal Peoples of Canada Gr. 7-8
SSK1-31	Addition & Subtraction Drills Gr. 1-3
SSK1-28	Addition Drills Gr. 1-3
SSY1-04	Addition Gr. 1-3
SSN1-174	Adv. of Huckle Berry Finn NS Gr. 7-8
SSB1-63	African Animals Gr 4-6
SSB1-29	All About Bears Gr. 1-2
SSF1-08	All About Boats Gr. 2-3
SSJ1-02	All About Canada Gr. 2
SSB1-54	All About Cattle Gr. 4-6
SSN1-10	All About Colours Gr. P-1
SSB1-93	All About Dinosaurs Gr. 2
SSN1-14	All About Dragons Gr. 3-5
SSB1-07	All About Elephants Gr. 3-4
SSB1-68	All About Fish Gr. 4-6
SSN1-39	All About Giants Gr. 2-3
SSH1-15	All About Jobs Gr. 1-3
SSH1-05	All About Me Gr. 1
SSA1-02	All About Mexico Gr. 4-6
SSR1-28	All About Nouns Gr. 5-7
SSF1-09	All About Planes Gr. 2-3
SSB1-33	All About Plants Gr. 2-3
SSR1-29	All About Pronouns Gr. 5-7
SSB1-12	All About Rabbits Gr. 2-3
SSB1-58	All About Spiders Gr. 4-6
SSA1-03	All About the Desert Gr. 4-6
SSA1-04	All About the Ocean Gr. 5-7
SSZ1-01	All About the Olympics Gr. 2-4
SSB1-49	All About the Sea Gr. 4-6
SSK1-06	All About Time Gr. 4-6
SSF1-07	All About Trains Gr. 2-3
SSH1-18	All About Transportation Gr. 2
SSB1-01	All About Trees Gr. 4-6
SSB1-61	All About Weather Gr. 7-8
SSB1-06	All About Whales Gr. 3-4
SSPC-26	All Kinds of Clocks B/W Pictures
SSB1-110	All Kinds of Structures Gr. 1
SSH1-19	All Kinds of Vehicles Gr. 3
SSF1-01	Amazing Aztecs Gr. 4-6
SSB1-92	Amazing Earthworms Gr. 2-3
SSJ1-50	Amazing Facts in Cdn History Gr. 4-6
SSB1-32	Amazing Insects Gr. 4-6
SSN1-132	Amelia Bedelia–Camping NS 1-3
SSN1-68	Amelia Bedelia NS 1-3
SSN1-155	Amelia Bedelia-Surprise Shower NS 1-3
SSA1-13	America The Beautiful Gr. 4-6
SSN1-57	Amish Adventure NS 7-8
SSF1-02	Ancient China Gr. 4-6
SSF1-18	Ancient Egypt Gr. 4-6
SSF1-21	Ancient Greece Gr. 4-6
SSF1-19	Ancient Rome Gr. 4-6
SSQ1-06	Animal Town – Big Book Pkg 1-3
SSQ1-02	Animals Prepare Winter – Big Book Pkg 1-3
SSN1-150	Animorphs the Invasion NS 4-6
SSN1-53	Anne of Green Gables NS 7-8
SSB1-40	Apple Celebration Gr. 4-6
SSB1-04	Apple Mania Gr. 2-3
SSB1-38	Apples are the Greatest Gr. P-K
SSB1-59	Arctic Animals Gr. 4-6
SSN1-162	Arnold Lobel Author Study Gr. 2-3
SSPC-22	Australia B/W Pictures
SSA1-05	Australia Gr. 5-8
SSM1-03	Autumn in the Woodlot Gr. 2-3
SSM1-08	Autumn Wonders Gr. 1
SSN1-41	Baby Sister for Frances NS 1-3
SSPC-19	Back to School B/W Pictures
SSC1-33	Back to School Gr. 2-3
SSN1-224	Banner in the Sky NS 7-8
SSN1-36	Bargain for Frances NS 1-3
SSB1-82	Bats Gr. 4-6
SSN1-71	BB – Drug Free Zone NS Gr. 1-3
SSN1-88	BB – In the Freaky House NS 1-3
SSN1-78	BB – Media Madness NS 1-3
SSN1-69	BB – Wheelchair Commando NS 1-3
SSN1-119	Be a Perfect Person-3 Days NS 4-6
SSC1-15	Be My Valentine Gr. 1
SSD1-01	Be Safe Not Sorry Gr. P-1

Code #	Title and Grade
SSN1-09	Bear Tales Gr. 2-4
SSB1-28	Bears Gr. 4-6
SSN1-202	Bears in Literature Gr. 1-3
SSN1-40	Beatrix Potter Gr. 2-4
SSN1-129	Beatrix Potter: Activity Biography Gr. 2-4
SSB1-47	Beautiful Bugs Gr. 1
SSB1-21	Beavers Gr. 3-5
SSN1-257	Because of Winn-Dixie NS Gr. 4-6
SSK1-04	Beginning Math Series: Calendar Gr. 2-3
SSR1-54	Beginning Cursive D. Gr. 2-4
SSR1-79	Beginning Cursive Z.B. Gr. 2-4
SSR1-53	Beginning Manuscript D. Gr. Pk-2
SSR1-76	Beginning Manuscript Z.B. Gr. PK-2
SSK1-08	Beginning Math Series: Shapes Gr. 1-3
SSK1-09	Beginning Math Series: Money CDN Gr. 1-3
SSK1-10	Beginning Math Series: Time Gr. 1-3
SSK1-22	Beginning Math Series: Measurement Gr. 1-3
SSK1-23	Beginning Math Series: Numbers Gr. 1-3
SSR1-58	Beginning and Practice Cursive D. Gr. 2-4
SSR1-82	Beginning and Practice Cursive Z.B. Gr. 2-4
SSR1-57	Beginning and Practice Manuscript D. Gr. PK-2
SSR1-83	Beginning and Practice Manuscript Z.B. Gr. Pk-2
SSN1-33	Bedtime for Frances NS 1-3
SSN1-114	Best Christmas Pageant Ever NS Gr. 4-6
SSN1-32	Best Friends for Frances NS Gr. 1-3
SSB1-39	Best Friends Pets Gr. P-K
SSN1-185	BFG NS Gr. 4-6
SSJ1-61	Big Book of Canadian Celebrations Gr. 1-3
SSJ1-62	Big Book of Canadian Celebrations Gr. 4-6
SSN1-35	Birthday for Frances NS Gr. 1-3
SSN1-107	Borrowers NS Gr. 4-6
SSC1-16	Bouquet of Valentines Gr. 2
SSN1-29	Bread & Jam for Frances NS Gr. 1-3
SSN1-63	Bridge to Terabithia NS Gr. 4-6
SSY1-24	BTS Numeración/Numeration Gr. 1-3
SSY1-25	BTS Adición/Addition Gr. 1-3
SSY1-26	BTS Sustracción/Subtraction Gr. 1-3
SSY1-27	BTS Fonética/Phonics Gr. 1-3
SSY1-28	BTS Leer para Entender/Reading for Understanding Gr. 1-3
SSY1-29	BTS Uso de las Mayúsculas y Reglas de Puntuación/Capitalization and Punctuation Gr. 1-3
SSY1-30	BTS Composición de Oraciones/ Sentence Writing Gr. 1-3
SSY1-31	BTS Composici13n de Historias/ Story Writing Gr. 1-3
SSN1-256	Bud, Not Buddy NS Gr. 4-6
SSB1-31	Bugs, Bugs & More Bugs Gr. 2-3
SSR1-07	Building Word Families L.V. Gr. 1-2
SSR1-05	Building Word Families S.V. Gr. 1-2
SSN1-204	Bunnicula NS Gr. 4-6
SSB1-80	Butterflies & Caterpillars Gr. 1-2
SSN1-164	Call It Courage NS Gr. 7-8
SSN1-67	Call of the Wild NS Gr. 7-8
SSJ1-41	Canada & It's Trading Partners 6-8
SSPC-28	Canada B/W Pictures
SSN1-173	Canada Geese Quilt NS Gr. 4-6
SSJ1-01	Canada Gr. 1
SSJ1-33	Canada's Capital Cities Gr. 4-6
SSJ1-43	Canada's Confederation Gr. 7-8
SSF1-04	Canada's First Nations Gr. 7-8
SSJ1-51	Canada's Landmarks Gr. 1-3
SSJ1-48	Canada's Landmarks Gr. 4-6
SSJ1-60	Canada's Links to the World Gr. 5-8
SSJ1-42	Canada's Traditions & Celeb. Gr. 1-3
SSB1-45	Canadian Animals Gr. 1-2
SSJ1-37	Canadian Arctic Inuit Gr. 2-3
SSJ1-53	Canadian Black History Gr. 4-8
SSJ1-57	Canadian Comprehension Gr. 1-2
SSJ1-58	Canadian Comprehension Gr. 3-4
SSJ1-59	Canadian Comprehension Gr. 5-6
SSJ1-46	Canadian Industries Gr. 4-6
SSK1-12	Canadian Problem Solving Gr. 4-6
SSJ1-38	Canadian Provinces & Terr. Gr. 4-6
SSY1-07	Capitalization & Punctuation Gr. 1-3
SSN1-198	Captain Courageous NS Gr. 7-8
SSK1-11	Cars Problem Solving Gr. 3-4

Code #	Title and Grade
SSN1-154	Castle in the Attic NS Gr. 4-6
SSF1-31	Castles & Kings Gr. 4-6
SSN1-144	Cat Ate My Gymsuit NS Gr. 4-6
SSPC-38	Cats B/W Pictures
SSB1-50	Cats – Domestic & Wild Gr. 4-6
SSN1-34	Cats in Literature Gr. 3-6
SSN1-212	Cay NS Gr. 7-8
SSM1-09	Celebrate Autumn Gr. 4-6
SSC1-39	Celebrate Christmas Gr. 4-6
SSC1-31	Celebrate Easter Gr. 4-6
SSC1-23	Celebrate Shamrock Day Gr. 2
SSM1-11	Celebrate Spring Gr. 4-6
SSC1-13	Celebrate Thanksgiving R. 3-4
SSM1-06	Celebrate Winter Gr. 4-6
SSB1-107	Cells, Tissues & Organs Gr. 7-8
SSB1-101	Characteristics of Flight Gr. 4-6
SSN1-66	Charlie & Chocolate Factory NS Gr. 4-6
SSN1-23	Charlotte's Web NS Gr. 4-6
SSB1-37	Chicks N'Ducks Gr. 2-4
SSA1-09	China Today Gr. 5-8
SSN1-70	Chocolate Fever NS Gr. 4-6
SSN1-241	Chocolate Touch NS Gr. 4-6
SSC1-38	Christmas Around the World Gr. 4-6
SSPC-42	Christmas B/W Pictures
SST1-08A	Christmas Gr. JK/SK
SST1-08B	Christmas Gr. 1
SST1-08C	Christmas Gr. 2-3
SSC1-04	Christmas Magic Gr. 1
SSC1-03	Christmas Tales Gr. 2-3
SSG1-06	Cinematography Gr. 5-8
SSPC-13	Circus B/W Pictures
SSF1-03	Circus Magic Gr. 3-4
SSJ1-52	Citizenship/Immigration Gr. 4-8
SSN1-104	Classical Poetry Gr. 7-12
SSN1-227	Color Gr. 1-3
SSN1-203	Colour Gr. 1-3
SSN1-135	Come Back Amelia Bedelia NS 1-3
SSH1-11	Community Helpers Gr. 1-3
SSK1-02	Concept Cards & Activities Gr. P-1
SSN1-183	Copper Sunrise NS Gr. 7-8
SSN1-86	Corduroy & Pocket Corduroy NS 1-3
SSN1-124	Could Dracula Live in Wood NS 4-6
SSN1-148	Cowboy's Don't Cry NS Gr. 7-8
SSR1-01	Creativity with Food Gr. 4-8
SSB1-34	Creatures of the Sea Gr. 2-4
SSN1-208	Curse of the Viking Grave NS 7-8
SSN1-134	Danny Champion of World NS 4-6
SSN1-98	Danny's Run NS Gr. 7-8
SSK1-21	Data Management Gr. 4-6
SSB1-53	Dealing with Dinosaurs Gr. 4-6
SSN1-178	Dear Mr. Henshaw NS Gr. 4-6
SSB1-22	Deer Gr. 3-5
SSPC-20	Desert B/W Pictures
SSJ1-40	Development of Western Canada 7-8
SSA1-16	Development of Manufacturing 7-9
SSN1-105	Dicken's Christmas NS Gr. 7-8
SSN1-62	Different Dragons NS Gr. 4-6
SSPC-21	Dinosaurs B/W Pictures
SSB1-16	Dinosaurs Gr. 1
SSB1-98	Dinosaurs Gr. 3
SST1-02A	Dinosaurs Gr. JK/SK
SST1-02B	Dinosaurs Gr. 1
SST1-02 C	Dinosaurs Gr. 2-3
SSN1-175	Dinosaurs in Literature Gr. 1-3
SSJ1-26	Discover Nova Scotia Gr. 5-7
SSJ1-36	Discover Nunavut Territory Gr. 5-7
SSJ1-25	Discover Ontario Gr. 5-7
SSJ1-24	Discover PEI Gr. 5-7
SSJ1-22	Discover Québec Gr. 5-7
SSL1-01	Discovering the Library Gr. 2-3
SSB1-106	Diversity of Living Things Gr. 4-6
SSK1-27	Division Drills Gr. 4-6
SSB1-30	Dogs – Wild & Tame Gr. 4-6
SSPC-31	Dogs B/W Pictures
SSN1-196	Dog's Don't Tell Jokes NS Gr. 4-6
SSN1-182	Door in the Wall NS Gr. 4-6
SSB1-87	Down by the Sea Gr. 1-3
SSN1-189	Dr. Jeckyll & Mr. Hyde NS Gr. 4-6
SSG1-07	Dragon Trivia Gr. P-8
SSN1-102	Dragon's Egg NS Gr. 4-6
SSN1-16	Dragons in Literature Gr. 3-6
SSC1-06	Early Christmas Gr. 3-5
SSB1-109	Earth's Crust Gr. 6-8
SSC1-21	Easter Adventures Gr. 3-4
SSC1-17	Easter Delights Gr. P-K
SSC1-19	Easter Surprises Gr. 1
SSPC-12	Egypt B/W Pictures
SSN1-255	Egypt Game NS Gr. 4-6
SSF1-28	Egyptians Today & Yesterday Gr. 2-3
SSJ1-49	Elections in Canada Gr. 4-8
SSB1-108	Electricity Gr. 4-6

Code #	Title and Grade
SSN1-02	Elves & the Shoemaker NS Gr. 1-3
SSH1-14	Emotions Gr. P-2
SSB1-85	Energy Gr. 4-6
SSN1-108	English Language Gr. 10-12
SSN1-156	Enjoying Eric Wilson Series Gr. 5-7
SSB1-64	Environment Gr. 4-6
SSR1-12	ESL Teaching Ideas Gr. K-8
SSN1-258	Esperanza Rising NS Gr. 4-6
SSR1-22	Exercises in Grammar Gr. 6
SSR1-23	Exercises in Grammar Gr. 7
SSR1-24	Exercises in Grammar Gr. 8
SSF1-20	Exploration Gr. 4-6
SSF1-15	Explorers & Mapmakers of Can. 7-8
SSJ1-54	Exploring Canada Gr. 1-3
SSJ1-56	Exploring Canada Gr. 1-6
SSJ1-55	Exploring Canada Gr. 4-6
SSH1-20	Exploring My School & Community 1
SSPC-39	Fables B/W Pictures
SSN1-15	Fables Gr. 4-6
SSN1-04	Fairy Tale Magic Gr. 3-5
SSPC-11	Fairy Tales B/W Pictures
SSN1-11	Fairy Tales Gr. 1-2
SSN1-199	Family Under the Bridge NS Gr. 4-6
SSPC-41	Famous Canadians B/W Pictures
SSJ1-12	Famous Canadians Gr. 4-8
SSN1-210	Fantastic Mr. Fox NS Gr. 4-6
SSB1-36	Fantastic Plants Gr. 4-6
SSPC-04	Farm Animals B/W Pictures
SSB1-15	Farm Animals Gr. 1-2
SST1-03A	Farm Gr. JK/SK
SST1-03B	Farm Gr. 1
SST1-03C	Farm Gr. 2-3
SSJ1-05	Farming Community Gr. 3-4
SSB1-44	Farmyard Friends Gr. P-K
SSJ1-45	Fathers of Confederation Gr. 4-8
SSB1-19	Feathered Friends Gr. 4-6
SST1-05A	February Gr. JK/SK
SST1-05B	February Gr. 1
SST1-05C	February Gr. 2-3
SSN1-03	Festival of Fairytales Gr. 3-5
SSC1-36	Festivals Around the World Gr. 2-3
SSN1-168	First 100 Sight Words Gr. 1
SSC1-32	First Days at School Gr. 1
SSJ1-06	Fishing Community Gr. 3-4
SSN1-170	Flowers for Algernon NS Gr. 7-8
SSN1-261	Flat Stanley NS Gr. 1-3
SSN1-128	Fly Away Home NS Gr. 4-6
SSD1-05	Food: Fact, Fun & Fiction Gr. 1-3
SSD1-06	Food: Nutrition & Invention Gr. 4-6
SSB1-118	Force and Motion Gr. 1-3
SSB1-119	Force and Motion Gr. 4-6
SSB1-25	Foxes Gr. 3-5
SSN1-263	Fractured Fairy Tales NS Gr. 1-3
SSN1-172	Freckle Juice NS Gr. 1-3
SSB1-43	Friendly Frogs Gr. 1
SSN1-260	Frindle NS Gr. 4-6
SSB1-89	Fruits & Seeds Gr. 4-6
SSN1-137	Fudge-a-Mania NS Gr. 4-6
SSB1-14	Fun on the Farm Gr. 3-4
SSR1-49	Fun with Phonics Gr. 1-3
SSPC-06	Garden Flowers B/W Pictures
SSK1-03	Geometric Shapes Gr. 2-5
SSC1-18	Get the Rabbit Habit Gr. 1-2
SSN1-209	Giver, The NS Gr. 7-8
SSN1-190	Go Jump in the Pool NS Gr. 4-6
SSG1-03	Goal Setting Gr. 6-8
SSG1-08	Gr. 3 Test – Parent Guide
SSG1-99	Gr. 3 Test – Teacher Guide
SSG1-09	Gr. 6 Language Test–Parent Guide
SSG1-97	Gr. 6 Language Test–Teacher Guide
SSG1-10	Gr. 6 Math Test – Parent Guide
SSG1-96	Gr. 6 Math Test – Teacher Guide
SSG1-98	Gr. 6 Math/Lang. Test–Teacher Guide
SSK1-14	Graph for all Seasons Gr. 1-3
SSN1-117	Great Brain NS Gr. 4-6
SSN1-90	Great Expectations NS Gr. 7-8
SSN1-169	Great Gilly Hopkins NS Gr. 4-6
SSN1-197	Great Science Fair Disaster NS Gr. 4-6
SSN1-138	Greek Mythology Gr. 7-8
SSN1-113	Green Gables Detectives NS 4-6
SSC1-26	Groundhog Celebration Gr. 2
SSC1-25	Groundhog Day Gr. 1
SSB1-113	Growth & Change in Animals Gr. 2-3
SSB1-114	Growth & Change in Plants Gr. 2-3
SSB1-48	Guinea Pigs & Friends Gr. 3-5
SSB1-104	Habitats Gr. 4-6
SSPC-18	Halloween B/W Pictures
SST1-04A	Halloween Gr. JK/SK
SST1-04B	Halloween Gr. 1
SST1-04C	Halloween Gr. 2-3
SSC1-10	Halloween Gr. 4-6

Page 1

H-07

Publication Listing

Code #	Title and Grade
SSC1-08	Halloween Happiness Gr. 1
SSC1-29	Halloween Spirits Gr. P-K
SSY1-13	Handwriting Manuscript Gr 1-3
SSY1-14	Handwriting Cursive Gr. 1-3
SSC1-42	Happy Valentines Day Gr. 3
SSN1-205	Harper Moon NS Gr. 7-8
SSN1-123	Harriet the Spy NS Gr. 4-6
SSC1-11	Harvest Time Wonders Gr. 1
SSN1-136	Hatchet NS Gr. 7-8
SSC1-09	Haunting Halloween Gr. 2-3
SSN1-91	Hawk & Stretch NS Gr. 4-6
SSC1-30	Hearts & Flowers Gr. P-K
SSN1-22	Heidi NS Gr. 4-6
SSN1-120	Help I'm Trapped in My NS Gr. 4-6
SSN1-24	Henry & the Clubhouse NS Gr. 4-6
SSN1-184	Hobbit NS Gr. 7-8
SSN1-122	Hoboken Chicken Emerg. NS 4-6
SSN1-250	Holes NS Gr. 4-6
SSN1-116	How Can a Frozen Detective NS 4-6
SSN1-89	How Can I be a Detective if I NS 4-6
SSN1-96	How Come the Best Clues... NS 4-6
SSN1-133	How To Eat Fried Worms NS Gr.4-6
SSR1-48	How To Give a Presentation Gr. 4-6
SSN1-125	How To Teach Writing Through 7-9
SSR1-10	How To Write a Composition 6-10
SSR1-09	How To Write a Paragraph 5-10
SSR1-08	How To Write an Essay Gr. 7-12
SSR1-03	How To Write Poetry & Stories 4-6
SSD1-07	Human Body Gr. 2-4
SSD1-02	Human Body Gr. 4-6
SSN1-25	I Want to Go Home NS Gr. 4-6
SSH1-06	I'm Important Gr. 2-3
SSH1-07	I'm Unique Gr. 4-6
SSF1-05	In Days of Yore Gr. 4-6
SSF1-06	In Pioneer Days Gr. 2-4
SSM1-10	In the Wintertime Gr. 2
SSB1-41	Incredible Dinosaurs Gr. P-1
SSN1-177	Incredible Journey NS Gr. 4-6
SSN1-100	Indian in the Cupboard NS Gr. 4-6
SSPC-05	Insects B/W Pictures
SSPC-10	Inuit B/W Pictures
SSJ1-10	Inuit Community Gr. 3-4
SSN1-85	Ira Sleeps Over NS Gr. 1-3
SSN1-93	Iron Man NS Gr. 4-6
SSN1-193	Island of the Blue Dolphins NS 4-6
SSB1-11	It's a Dogs World Gr. 2-3
SSM1-05	It's a Marshmallow World Gr. 3
SSK1-05	It's About Time Gr. 2-4
SSC1-41	It's Christmas Time Gr. 3
SSH1-04	It's Circus Time Gr. 1
SSC1-43	It's Groundhog Day Gr. 3
SSB1-75	It's Maple Syrup Time Gr. 2-4
SSC1-40	It's Trick or Treat Time Gr. 2
SSN1-65	James & The Giant Peach NS 4-6
SSN1-106	Jane Eyre NS Gr. 7-8
SSPC-25	Japan B/W Pictures
SSA1-06	Japan Gr. 5-8
SSN1-264	Journey to the Centre of the Earth NS Gr. 7-8
SSC1-05	Joy of Christmas Gr. 2
SSN1-161	Julie of the Wolves NS Gr. 7-8
SSB1-81	Jungles Gr. 2-3
SSE1-02	Junior Music for Fall Gr. 4-6
SSE1-05	Junior Music for Spring Gr. 4-6
SSE1-06	Junior Music for Winter Gr. 4-6
SSR1-62	Just for Boys - Reading Comprehension Gr. 3-6
SSR1-63	Just for Boys - Reading Comprehension Gr. 6-8
SSN1-151	Kate NS Gr. 4-6
SSN1-95	Kidnapped in the Yukon NS Gr. 4-6
SSN1-140	Kids at Bailey School Gr. 2-4
SSN1-176	King of the Wind NS Gr. 4-6
SSF1-29	Klondike Gold Rush Gr. 4-6
SSF1-33	Labour Movement in Canada Gr. 7-8
SSN1-152	Lamplighter NS Gr. 4-6
SSN1-38	Learning About Giants Gr. 4-6
SSB1-46	Learning About Mice Gr. 3-5
SSH1-17	Learning About Transportation Gr. 1
SSB1-02	Leaves Gr. 2-3
SSN1-50	Legends Gr. 4-6
SSC1-27	Lest We Forget Gr. 4-6
SSJ1-13	Let's Look at Canada Gr. 4-6
SSJ1-16	Let's Visit Alberta Gr. 2-4
SSJ1-15	Let's Visit British Columbia Gr. 2-4
SSJ1-03	Let's Visit Canada Gr. 3
SSJ1-18	Let's Visit Manitoba Gr. 2-4
SSJ1-21	Let's Visit New Brunswick Gr. 2-4
SSJ1-27	Let's Visit NFLD & Labrador Gr. 2-4
SSJ1-30	Let's Visit North West Terr. Gr. 2-4
SSJ1-20	Let's Visit Nova Scotia Gr. 2-4
SSJ1-34	Let's Visit Nunavut Gr. 2-4
SSJ1-17	Let's Visit Ontario Gr. 2-4
SSQ1-08	Let's Visit Ottawa Big Book Pkg 1-3
SSJ1-19	Let's Visit PEI Gr. 2-4
SSJ1-31	Let's Visit Québec Gr. 2-4
SSJ1-14	Let's Visit Saskatchewan Gr. 2-4
SSJ1-28	Let's Visit Yukon Gr. 2-4
SSN1-130	Life & Adv. of Santa Claus NS 7-8
SSB1-10	Life in a Pond Gr. 3-4
SSF1-30	Life in the Middle Ages Gr. 7-8
SSB1-103	Light & Sound Gr. 4-6
SSN1-219	Light in the Forest NS Gr. 7-8
SSN1-121	Light on Hogback Hill NS Gr. 4-6
SSN1-46	Lion, Witch & the Wardrobe NS 4-6
SSR1-51	Literature Response Forms Gr. 1-3
SSR1-52	Literature Response Forms Gr. 4-6
SSN1-28	Little House Big Woods NS 4-6
SSN1-233	Little House on the Prairie NS 4-6
SSN1-111	Little Women NS Gr. 7-8
SSN1-115	Live from the Fifth Grade NS 4-6
SSN1-141	Look Through My Window NS 4-6
SSN1-112	Look! Visual Discrimination Gr. P-1
SSN1-269	Loser NS Gr. 4-6
SSN1-61	Lost & Found NS Gr. 4-6
SSN1-109	Lost in the Barrens NS Gr. 7-8
SSJ1-08	Lumbering Community Gr. 3-4
SSN1-167	Magic School Bus Gr. 1-3
SSN1-247	Magic Treehouse Gr. 1-3
SSB1-78	Magnets Gr. 3-5
SSD1-03	Making Sense of Our Senses K-1
SSN1-146	Mama's Going to Buy You a NS 4-6
SSB1-94	Mammals Gr. 1
SSB1-95	Mammals Gr. 2
SSB1-96	Mammals Gr. 3
SSB1-97	Mammals Gr. 5-6
SSN1-160	Maniac Magee NS Gr. 4-6
SSA1-19	Mapping Activities & Outlines! 4-8
SSA1-17	Mapping Skills Gr. 1-3
SSA1-07	Mapping Skills Gr. 4-6
SST1-10A	March Gr. JK/SK
SST1-10B	March Gr. 1
SST1-10C	March Gr. 2-3
SSB1-57	Marvellous Marsupials Gr. 4-6
SSK1-01	Math Signs & Symbols Gr. 1-3
SSB1-116	Matter & Materials Gr. 1-3
SSB1-117	Matter & Materials Gr. 4-6
SSH1-03	Me, I'm Special! Gr. P-1
SSK1-16	Measurement Gr. 4-8
SSC1-02	Medieval Christmas Gr. 4-6
SSPC-09	Medieval Life B/W Pictures
SSC1-07	Merry Christmas Gr. P-K
SSK1-15	Metric Measurement Gr. 4-8
SSN1-13	Mice in Literature Gr. 3-5
SSB1-70	Microscopy Gr. 4-6
SSN1-180	Midnight Fox NS Gr. 4-6
SSN1-243	Midwife's Apprentice NS Gr. 4-6
SSJ1-07	Mining Community Gr. 3-4
SSN1-266	Missing May NS Gr. 4-6
SSK1-17	Money Talks – Cdn Gr. 3-6
SSK1-18	Money Talks – USA Gr. 3-6
SSB1-56	Monkeys & Apes Gr. 4-6
SSN1-43	Monkeys in Literature Gr. 2-4
SSN1-54	Monster Mania Gr. 4-6
SSN1-97	Mouse & the Motorcycle NS 4-6
SSN1-94	Mr. Poppers Penguins NS Gr. 4-6
SSN1-201	Mrs. Frisby & Rats NS Gr. 4-6
SSR1-13	Milti-Level Spelling Program Gr. 3-6
SSR1-26	Multi-Level Spelling USA Gr. 3-6
SSK1-31	Addition & Subtraction Drills 1-3
SSK1-32	Multiplication & Division Drills 4-6
SSK1-30	Multiplication Drills Gr. 4-6
SSA1-14	My Country! The USA! Gr. 2-4
SSN1-186	My Side of the Mountain NS 7-8
SSN1-58	Mysteries, Monsters & Magic Gr. 6-8
SSN1-37	Mystery at Blackrock Island NS 7-8
SSN1-80	Mystery House NS 4-6
SSN1-157	Nate the Great & Sticky Case NS 1-3
SSF1-23	Native People of North America 4-6
SSF1-25	New France Part 1 Gr. 7-8
SSF1-27	New France Part 2 Gr. 7-8
SSA1-10	New Zealand Gr. 4-8
SSN1-51	Newspapers Gr. 5-8
SSN1-47	No Word for Goodbye NS Gr. 7-8
SSPC-03	North American Animals B/W Pictures
SSF1-22	North American Natives Gr. 2-4
SSN1-75	Novel Ideas Gr. 4-6
SST1-06A	November JK/SK
SST1-06B	November Gr. 1
SST1-06C	November Gr. 2-3
SSN1-244	Number the Stars NS Gr. 4-6
SSY1-03	Numeration Gr. 1-3
SSPC-14	Nursery Rhymes B/W Pictures
SSN1-12	Nursery Rhymes Gr. P-1
SSN1-59	On the Banks of Plum Creek NS 4-6
SSN1-220	One in Middle Green Kangaroo NS 1-3
SSN1-145	One to Grow On NS Gr. 4-6
SSB1-27	Opossums Gr. 3-5
SSJ1-23	Ottawa Gr. 7-9
SSJ1-39	Our Canadian Governments Gr. 5-8
SSF1-14	Our Global Heritage Gr. 4-6
SSH1-12	Our Neighbourhoods Gr. 4-6
SSB1-72	Our Trash Gr. 2-3
SSB1-51	Our Universe Gr. 5-8
SSB1-86	Outer Space Gr. 1-2
SSA1-18	Outline Maps of the World Gr. 1-8
SSB1-67	Owls Gr. 4-6
SSN1-31	Owls in the Family NS Gr. 4-6
SSL1-02	Oxbridge Owl & The Library Gr. 4-6
SSB1-71	Pandas, Polar & Penguins Gr. 4-6
SSN1-52	Paperbag Princess NS Gr. 1-3
SSR1-11	Passion of Jesus: A Play Gr. 7-8
SSA1-12	Passport to Adventure Gr. 4-5
SSR1-06	Passport to Adventure Gr. 7-8
SSR1-04	Personal Spelling Dictionary Gr. 2-5
SSPC-29	Pets B/W Pictures
SSE1-03	Phantom of the Opera Gr. 7-9
SSN1-171	Phoebe Gilman Author Study Gr. 2-3
SSY1-06	Phonics Gr. 1-3
SSK1-33	Picture Math Book Gr. 1-3
SSN1-237	Pierre Berton Author Study Gr. 7-8
SSN1-179	Pigman NS Gr. 7-8
SSN1-48	Pigs in Literature Gr. 2-4
SSN1-99	Pinballs NS Gr. 4-6
SSN1-60	Pippi Longstocking NS Gr. 4-6
SSF1-12	Pirates Gr. 4-6
SSK1-13	Place Value Gr. 4-6
SSB1-77	Planets Gr. 3-6
SSR1-74	Poetry Prompts Gr. 1-3
SSR1-75	Poetry Prompts Gr. 4-6
SSB1-66	Popcorn Fun Gr. 2-3
SSB1-20	Porcupines Gr. 3-5
SSR1-56	Practice Cursive D. Gr. 2-4
SSR1-81	Practice Cursive Z.B. Gr. 2-4
SSR1-55	Practice Manuscript D. Gr. Pk-2
SSR1-80	Practice Manuscript Z.B. Gr. Pk-2
SSF1-24	Prehistoric Times Gr. 4-6
SSE1-01	Primary Music for Fall Gr. 1-3
SSE1-04	Primary Music for Spring Gr. 1-3
SSE1-07	Primary Music for Winter Gr. 1-3
SSJ1-47	Prime Ministers of Canada Gr. 4-8
SSN1-262	Prince Caspian NS Gr. 4-6
SSK1-20	Probability & Inheritance Gr. 7-10
SSN1-49	Question of Loyalty NS Gr. 7-8
SSN1-26	Rabbits in Literature Gr. 2-4
SSB1-17	Raccoons Gr. 3-5
SSN1-207	Radio Fifth Grade NS Gr. 4-6
SSB1-52	Rainbow of Colours Gr. 4-6
SSN1-144	Ramona Quimby Age 8 NS 4-6
SSJ1-09	Ranching Community Gr. 3-4
SSY1-08	Reading for Meaning Gr. 1-3
SSR1-76	Reading Logs Gr. K-1
SSR1-77	Reading Logs Gr. 2-3
SSN1-165	Reading Response Forms Gr. 1-3
SSN1-239	Reading Response Forms Gr. 4-6
SSN1-234	Reading with Arthur Gr. 1-3
SSN1-249	Reading with Canadian Authors 1-3
SSN1-200	Reading with Curious George Gr. 2-4
SSN1-230	Reading with Eric Carle Gr. 1-3
SSN1-251	Reading with Kenneth Oppel Gr. 4-6
SSN1-127	Reading with Mercer Mayer Gr. 1-2
SSN1-07	Reading with Motley Crew Gr. 2-3
SSN1-142	Reading with Robert Munsch 1-3
SSN1-06	Reading with the Super Sleuths 4-6
SSN1-08	Reading with the Ziggles Gr. 1
SST1-11A	Red Gr. JK/SK
SSN1-147	Refuge NS Gr. 7-8
SSC1-44	Remembrance Day Gr. 1-3
SSPC-23	Reptiles B/W Pictures
SSB1-42	Reptiles Gr. 4-6
SSN1-110	Return of the Indian NS Gr. 4-6
SSN1-225	River NS Gr. 7-8
SSE1-08	Robert Schuman, Composer Gr. 6-9
SSN1-83	Robot Alert NS Gr. 4-6
SSB1-65	Rocks & Minerals Gr. 4-6
SSB1-69	Rocks & Soils Gr. 2-3
SSN1-149	Romeo & Juliet NS Gr. 7-8
SSB1-88	Romping Reindeer Gr. K-3
SSN1-21	Rumplestiltskin NS Gr. 1-3
SSN1-153	Runaway Ralph NS Gr. 4-6
SSN1-103	Sadako & 1000 Paper Cranes NS 4-6
SSD1-04	Safety Gr. 2-4
SSN1-42	Sarah Plain & Tall NS Gr. 4-6
SSC1-34	School in September Gr. 4-6
SSPC-01	Sea Creatures B/W Pictures
SSB1-79	Sea Creatures Gr. 1-3
SSN1-64	Secret Garden NS Gr. 4-6
SSB1-90	Seeds & Weeds Gr. 2-3
SSY1-02	Sentence Writing Gr. 1-3
SST1-07A	September JK/SK
SST1-07B	September Gr. 1
SST1-07C	September Gr. 2-3
SSN1-30	Serendipity Series Gr. 3-5
SSC1-22	Shamrocks on Parade Gr. 1
SSC1-24	Shamrocks, Harps & Shillelaghs 3-4
SSR1-66	Shakespeare Shorts-Perf Arts Gr. 1-4
SSR1-67	Shakespeare Shorts-Perf Arts Gr. 4-6
SSR1-68	Shakespeare Shorts-Lang Arts Gr. 2-4
SSR1-69	Shakespeare Shorts-Lang Arts Gr. 4-6
SSB1-74	Sharks Gr. 4-6
SSN1-158	Shiloh NS Gr. 4-6
SSN1-84	Sideways Stories Wayside NS 4-6
SSN1-181	Sight Words Activities Gr. 1
SSB1-100	Simple Machines Gr. 1-3
SSB1-99	Simple Machines Gr. 4-6
SSN1-19	Sixth Grade Secrets 4-6
SSG1-04	Skill Building with Slates Gr. K-8
SSN1-118	Skinny Bones NS Gr. 4-6
SSB1-24	Skunks Gr. 3-5
SSN1-191	Sky is Falling NS Gr. 4-6
SSB1-83	Slugs & Snails Gr. 1-3
SSB1-55	Snakes Gr. 4-6
SST1-12A	Snow Gr. JK/SK
SST1-12B	Snow Gr. 1
SST1-12C	Snow Gr. 2-3
SSB1-76	Solar System Gr. 4-6
SSPC-44	South America B/W Pictures
SSA1-11	South America Gr. 4-6
SSB1-05	Space Gr. 2-3
SSR1-34	Spelling Blacklines Gr. 1
SSR1-35	Spelling Blacklines Gr. 2
SSR1-36	Spelling Blacklines Gr. 3
SSR1-37	Spelling Blacklines Gr. 4
SSR1-14	Spelling Gr. 1
SSR1-15	Spelling Gr. 2
SSR1-16	Spelling Gr. 3
SSR1-17	Spelling Gr. 4
SSR1-18	Spelling Gr. 5
SSR1-19	Spelling Gr. 6
SSR1-27	Spelling Worksavers #1 Gr. 3-5
SSM1-02	Spring Celebration Gr. 2-3
SST1-01A	Spring Gr. JK/SK
SST1-01B	Spring Gr. 1
SST1-01C	Spring Gr. 2-3
SSM1-01	Spring in the Garden Gr. 1-2
SSB1-26	Squirrels Gr. 3-5
SSB1-112	Stable Structures & Mechanisms 3
SSG1-05	Steps in the Research Process 5-8
SSG1-02	Stock Market Gr. 7-8
SSN1-139	Stone Fox NS Gr. 4-6
SSN1-214	Stone Orchard NS Gr. 7-8
SSN1-01	Story Book Land of Witches Gr. 2-3
SSR1-64	Story Starters Gr. 1-3
SSR1-65	Story Starters Gr. 4-6
SSR1-73	Story Starters Gr. 1-6
SSY1-09	Story Writing Gr. 1-3
SSB1-111	Structures, Mechanisms & Motion 2
SSN1-211	Stuart Little NS Gr. 4-6
SSK1-29	Subtraction Drills Gr. 1-3
SSY1-05	Subtraction Gr. 1-3
SSY1-11	Successful Language Pract. Gr. 1-3
SSY1-12	Successful Math Practice Gr. 1-3
SSW1-09	Summer Learning Gr. K-1
SSW1-10	Summer Learning Gr. 1-2
SSW1-11	Summer Learning Gr. 2-3
SSW1-12	Summer Learning Gr. 3-4
SSW1-13	Summer Learning Gr. 4-5
SSW1-14	Summer Learning Gr. 5-6
SSN1-159	Summer of the Swans NS Gr. 4-6
SSZ1-02	Summer Olympics Gr. 4-6
SSM1-07	Super Summer Gr. 1-2
SSN1-18	Superfudge NS Gr. 4-6
SSA1-08	Switzerland Gr. 4-6
SSN1-20	T.V. Kid NS. Gr. 4-6
SSA1-15	Take a Trip to Australia Gr. 2-3
SSB1-102	Taking Off With Flight Gr. 1-3
SSK1-34	Teaching Math with Everyday Munipulatives Gr. 4-6
SSN1-259	The Tale of Despereaux NS Gr. 4-6
SSN1-265	The Breadwinner NS Gr. 4-6
SSN1-55	Tales of the Fourth Grade NS 4-6
SSN1-188	Taste of Blackberries NS Gr. 4-6
SSK1-07	Teaching Math Through Sports 6-9
SST1-09A	Thanksgiving JK/SK
SST1-09C	Thanksgiving Gr. 2-3
SSN1-77	There's a Boy in the Girls... NS 4-6
SSN1-143	This Can't Be Happening NS 4-6

Page 2

Publication Listing

Code #	Title and Grade
SSN1-05	Three Billy Goats Gruff NS Gr. 1-3
SSN1-72	Ticket to Curlew NS Gr. 4-6
SSN1-82	Timothy of the Cay NS Gr. 7-8
SSF1-32	Titanic Gr. 4-6
SSN1-222	To Kill a Mockingbird NS Gr. 7-8
SSN1-195	Toilet Paper Tigers NS Gr. 4-6
SSJ1-35	Toronto Gr. 4-8
SSH1-02	Toy Shelf Gr. P-K
SSPC-24	Toys B/W Pictures
SSN1-163	Traditional Poetry Gr. 7-10
SSH1-13	Transportation Gr. 4-6
SSW1-01	Transportation Snip Art
SSB1-03	Trees Gr. 2-3
SSA1-01	Tropical Rainforest Gr. 4-6
SSN1-56	Trumpet of the Swan NS Gr. 4-6
SSN1-81	Tuck Everlasting NS Gr. 4-6
SSN1-126	Turtles in Literature Gr. 1-3
SSN1-45	Underground to Canada NS 4-6
SSN1-27	Unicorns in Literature Gr. 3-5
SSJ1-44	Upper & Lower Canada Gr. 7-8
SSN1-192	Using Novels Canadian North Gr. 7-8
SSC1-14	Valentines Day Gr. 5-8
SSPC-45	Vegetables B/W Pictures
SSY1-01	Very Hungry Caterpillar NS 30/Pkg Gr. 1-3
SSF1-13	Victorian Era Gr. 7-8
SSC1-35	Victorian Christmas Gr. 5-8
SSF1-17	Viking Age Gr. 4-6
SSN1-206	War with Grandpa SN Gr. 4-6
SSB1-91	Water Gr. 2-4
SSN1-166	Watership Down NS Gr. 7-8
SSH1-16	Ways We Travel Gr. P-K
SSN1-101	Wayside Sch. Little Stranger NS Gr. 4-6
SSN1-76	Wayside Sch. is Falling Down NS 4-6
SSB1-60	Weather Gr. 4-6
SSN1-17	Wee Folk in Literature Gr. 3-5
SSPC-08	Weeds B/W Pictures
SSQ1-04	Welcome Back – Big Book Pkg 1-3
SSB1-73	Whale Preservation Gr. 5-8
SSH1-08	What is a Community? Gr. 2-4
SSH1-01	What is a Family? Gr. 2-3
SSH1-09	What is a School? Gr. 1-2
SSJ1-32	What is Canada? Gr. P-K
SSN1-79	What is RAD? Read & Discover 2-4
SSB1-62	What is the Weather Today? Gr. 2-4
SSN1-194	What's a Daring Detective NS 4-6
SSH1-10	What's My Number Gr. P-K
SSR1-02	What's the Scoop on Words Gr. 4-6
SSN1-73	Where the Red Fern Grows NS Gr. 7-8
SSN1-87	Where the Wild Things Are NS Gr. 1-3
SSN1-187	Whipping Boy NS Gr. 4-6
SSN1-226	Who is Frances Rain? NS Gr. 4-6
SSN1-74	Who's Got Gertie & How...? NS Gr. 4-6
SSN1-131	Why did the Underwear ... NS 4-6
SSC1-28	Why Wear a Poppy? Gr. 2-3
SSJ1-11	Wild Animals of Canada Gr. 2-3
SSPC-07	Wild Flowers B/W Pictures
SSB1-18	Winter Birds Gr. 2-3
SSZ1-03	Winter Olympics Gr. 4-6
SSM1-04	Winter Wonderland Gr. 1
SSC1-01	Witches Gr. 3-4
SSN1-213	Wolf Island NS Gr. 1-3
SSE1-09	Wolfgang Amadeus Mozart 6-9
SSB1-23	Wolves Gr. 3-5
SSC1-20	Wonders of Easter Gr. 2
SSY1-15	Word Families Gr. 1-3
SSR1-59	Word Families 2,3 Letter Words Gr. 1-3
SSR1-60	Word Families 3, 4 Letter Words Gr. 1-3
SSR1-61	Word Families 2, 3, 4 Letter Words Big Book Gr. 1-3
SSB1-35	World of Horses Gr. 4-6
SSB1-13	World of Pets Gr. 2-3
SSF1-26	World War II Gr. 7-8
SSN1-221	Wrinkle in Time NS Gr. 7-8
SSPC-02	Zoo Animals B/W Pictures
SSB1-08	Zoo Animals Gr. 1-2
SSB1-09	Zoo Celebration Gr. 3-4